BREAK FREE FROM YOUR OCD

A TEEN'S PATH TO PEACE AND FREEDOM

PROVEN STRATEGIES AND PRACTICAL TOOLS TO HELP
YOU CONQUER YOUR FEARS, REGAIN CONTROL, AND
LIVE FREE FROM OCD

RICK BRYANT

This book is dedicated to everyone on the path to healing, growth, and self-discovery. May these words provide you with the tools and encouragement to find peace and freedom within yourself. To those who face their challenges with courage and resilience—you are not alone. This journey is yours, and I'm honored to be a part of it.

Rick Bryant

The curious paradox is that when I accept myself just as I am, then I can change.

— CARL ROGERS

Even a happy life cannot be without a measure of darkness, and the word happy would lose its meaning if it were not balanced by sadness.

— CARL JUNG

The most beautiful people we have known are those who have known defeat, known suffering, known struggle, known loss, and have found their way out of the depths. These persons have an appreciation, a sensitivity, and an understanding of life that fills them with compassion, gentleness, and a deep loving concern. Beautiful people do not just happen.

— ELISABETH KÜBLER-ROSS

If you have been brutally broken, but still have the courage to be gentle to other living beings, then you're a badass with the heart of an angel.

— KEANU REEVES

CONTENTS

INTRODUCTION

Let me tell you about Jake. Jake is a 16-year-old high school student who loves playing guitar and hanging out with his friends. But Jake also battles something that many don't see. He spends hours checking and rechecking his homework, washing his hands until they're raw, and repeating certain phrases in his head to ward off bad luck. These rituals are not quirks or habits; they are symptoms of OCD (Obsessive-Compulsive Disorder). Jake often feels trapped in a cycle of relentless thoughts and actions and is not alone.

This book, "Break Free from Your OCD: A Teen's Path to Peace and Freedom," aims to offer a lifeline to teens like Jake. The purpose is simple yet profound: to provide proven strategies and practical tools that help you regain control and live free from OCD. We'll explore evidence-based approaches like Cognitive Behavioral Therapy (CBT), Dialectical Behavior Therapy (DBT), Acceptance and Commitment Therapy (ACT), and the Triple-A Response®. These methods are not just buzzwords; they are effective techniques that have helped countless individuals manage their OCD.

My name is Rick Bryant, and I've spent decades working with individuals to improve their mental and emotional well-being. Throughout my career as a nurse and mental health advocate, I've seen firsthand how OCD can deeply affect daily life. This book is born out of my passion for helping people find relief, peace, and ultimately regain control over their lives.

The tools and strategies you'll find here are based on real-world experience and tailored to provide practical support and effective solutions. Whether you're working to gain better control over your OCD or seeking lasting relief from its challenges, this book offers practical tools to help you find peace and freedom. My hope is that this book will serve as a guide to overcoming the challenges of OCD and finding your way to a life of greater joy and freedom.

Understanding OCD in teens is crucial. According to the International OCD Foundation, about 1 in 100 children and teens have OCD, which means that in a school of 1,000 students, at least 10 students may be struggling with this condition. OCD is more than just being tidy or having peculiar habits. It involves obsessive thoughts and compulsive actions that can severely disrupt daily life. The Anxiety and Depression Association of America states that OCD is often accompanied by other mental health issues such as anxiety and depression. This makes it even more important to address OCD holistically.

So, what sets this book apart? It's not just a manual; it's a companion. You'll find step-by-step guidance on how to apply complex therapeutic techniques in ways that are easy to understand and follow. We'll delve into mindfulness and meditation practices that can help free you from obsessive thoughts and compulsive behaviors. You'll learn about the SMART Goals framework, which helps you set realistic and achievable goals, building confidence as you track your progress. Plus, we have real-life stories from teens who have successfully managed their OCD, offering hope and motivation.

This book is for teens who are struggling with OCD and their families who wish to support them. It's also for educators, counselors, and anyone who wants to better understand OCD. The interactive exercises, journaling prompts, and reflective activities are designed to foster self-awareness, reduce anxiety, and enhance problem-solving skills. Parents will find a dedicated section offering guidance on supporting their teen's OCD management while maintaining healthy family relationships.

The book is structured to be both informative and engaging. Each chapter focuses on a specific aspect of managing OCD, from understanding the condition to applying therapeutic techniques and setting goals. At the end of each chapter, case studies provide inspiration and practical insights. These stories show that while OCD can be challenging, it is manageable with the right tools and mindset.

Throughout this book, you'll encounter interactive worksheets and exercises designed to make the learning process active and engaging. These activities will help you apply what you've learned and track your progress. The goal is to make this journey as interactive and practical as possible.

So, I invite you to dive in. Read, reflect, and engage with the exercises. This book is here to support you every step of the way. You have the power to break free from OCD and reclaim your life. Let's start this journey together.

Rick Bryant

UNDERSTANDING OCD AND ITS IMPACT

Have you ever met someone who can't leave the house without checking if the door is locked five times, even when they know it's already locked? Or you know someone who washes their hands so often that their skin gets dry and cracked. These are not just quirky habits; they might be signs of OCD, a condition that can take over someone's life in ways that are hard to understand if you haven't experienced it yourself.

This chapter aims to explain OCD, how it differs from other anxiety disorders, and why it's so important to recognize and treat it early. We'll explore the basics of OCD, examine some statistics to understand its impact, and discuss why getting help sooner rather than later can make a big difference.

WHAT IS OCD? BREAKING DOWN THE BASICS

OCD stands for Obsessive-Compulsive Disorder. It's a mental health disorder that involves two main components: obsessions and compulsions. Obsessions are intrusive thoughts, images, or urges that pop into your mind and are extremely hard to ignore. These thoughts can be about anything—germs, harm, symmetry, or something completely different. Compulsions, on the other hand, are the repetitive behaviors or mental acts you feel driven to perform in response to these obsessions. These actions are meant to reduce the anxiety caused by the obsessions, but they usually end up making things worse in the long run.

Imagine you're sitting in class, trying to focus on a lesson. Suddenly, you get this overwhelming thought that if you don't tap your foot ten times, something terrible will happen to your family. You know this thought doesn't make any sense, but the anxiety it causes is so real that you can't help but give in and tap your foot. This is how OCD affects daily life. It turns everyday activities into a battlefield of anxious thoughts and repetitive actions.

OCD is more common than you might think, and it's definitely treatable. According to the International OCD Foundation, about 1 in 100 children and teens have OCD, which means that in a typical high school, several students might be dealing with this condition. The Anxiety and Depression Association of America notes that OCD often starts in childhood or adolescence, and early diagnosis and treatment are crucial for effective management.

It's important to understand how OCD differs from other anxiety disorders, like Generalized Anxiety Disorder (GAD). While both involve anxiety, they manifest differently. GAD is characterized by excessive worry about everyday things like school, friendships, or future events. OCD, on the other hand, specifically involves obsessions and compulsions. For example, someone with GAD might worry constantly about their grades, while someone with OCD might have an intrusive thought about germs and feel compelled to wash their hands repeatedly.

A common misconception is thinking that being neat or organized means you have OCD. People might say, "I'm so OCD about my room," when they just like things tidy. This trivializes the condition and overlooks the intense anxiety and disruption that real OCD causes. It's not about being neat; it's about feeling an overwhelming compulsion to perform actions that don't make sense but feel impossible to resist.

To put things in perspective, about 2-3% of people worldwide have OCD, which includes many teens. The average age of onset is around 10, but it can start earlier or later. Common teen triggers include stress from school, social situations, or family dynamics. Recognizing these triggers early can make a huge difference in managing the condition effectively.

Early recognition and treatment of OCD are essential. The sooner you identify the signs, the sooner you can start managing them. Early intervention can prevent OCD from interfering with your school, social life, and overall well-being. Common signs to watch for include repeated hand-washing, checking things multiple times, or needing things to be symmetrical or in a specific order. If you notice these behaviors in yourself or a friend, seeking help is important. Therapies like CBT and ERP have been proven effective in managing OCD symptoms.

So, as we dive deeper into understanding OCD, remember that recognizing and addressing it early can lead to better outcomes. Don't hesitate to seek help if you feel overwhelmed by intrusive thoughts and compulsive behaviors. You have the power to take control and live a life less dominated by OCD.

HOW OCD MANIFESTS: REAL-LIFE TEEN STORIES

Let's talk about Emma. Emma is a bright, energetic teenager who loves science and dreams of becoming a doctor. But Emma's life is overshadowed by her intense fear of germs. She spends hours each day washing her hands, scrubbing them until they bleed. She avoids touching doorknobs and uses her elbows to open doors, which makes her classmates look at her strangely. Emma's contamination fears are so overpowering that she can't focus in class and often misses school activities. Her hands are raw from the constant washing, and she feels isolated because she can't explain her behavior to her friends. Emma's story highlights the emotional and physical toll that OCD can take on someone's life.

Then there's Jake. Jake is a 15-year-old who loves playing video games and hanging out with his friends. But Jake's mind is often invaded by intrusive thoughts about harming others. These thoughts are horrifying and make him feel like a terrible person, even though he knows he would never act on them. Jake has developed rituals like counting and repeating certain phrases in his head to cope. He believes these actions will prevent something bad from happening. The stress of these thoughts and rituals makes it hard for Jake to concentrate on his schoolwork or enjoy time with friends. He feels a constant sense of dread and guilt, which has severely impacted his self-esteem.

Lily is another example. She's a star athlete who excels in school but struggles with checking behaviors. Before leaving the house, she spends an hour ensuring all the lights are off, the doors are locked, and her school bag is perfectly packed. She checks and rechecks her homework to the point where she often stays up late, leaving her exhausted the next day. These rituals make her late for school and sports practice, causing friction with her teachers and coaches. Lily feels embarrassed and stressed, fearing that people will think she's lazy or irresponsible. Her checking behaviors control her life, making it difficult for her to enjoy her accomplishments.

Alex's experience is different but just as challenging. Alex has a need for symmetry and order. Objects in his room must be perfectly aligned, and his clothes must be arranged by color and type. If something is out of place, Alex experiences intense anxiety until he can fix it. This need for order extends to his schoolwork, where he will rewrite notes and assignments multiple times to ensure they are perfect. These compulsions consume a significant amount of his time, making it hard to keep up with schoolwork and socialize with friends. Alex feels trapped by his need for perfection and worries that he'll never be able to relax.

These stories illustrate the diversity of OCD symptoms. One person might be obsessed with cleanliness, while another is plagued by intrusive thoughts or the need for order. For some, the compulsions are visible behaviors like hand-washing or checking locks. For others, they are mental rituals like counting or repeating phrases. The variety of symptoms means that everyone's experience with OCD is unique, but the impact on daily life is often profound.

The emotional impact of OCD is significant. Feelings of shame and embarrassment are common, as teens often recognize that their behaviors are irrational but feel powerless to stop them. The anxiety and stress levels can be overwhelming, leading to difficulties in focusing on schoolwork and maintaining friendships. OCD can erode self-esteem and confidence, making teens feel like they are constantly battling an invisible enemy.

OCD also affects daily activities in numerous ways. Completing homework can become an ordeal because of the time-consuming rituals involved. Social life suffers as teens might avoid situations where they fear their compulsions will be noticed or judged. Family dynamics can become strained as parents and siblings struggle to understand the behaviors, leading to conflicts and misunderstandings.

These real-life examples show how varied and disruptive OCD can be. Whether it's dealing with contamination fears like Emma, battling intrusive thoughts like Jake, managing checking behaviors like Lily, or overcoming the need for order like Alex, OCD is a multifaceted condition that affects every aspect of life. Understanding these experiences can help us empathize with those who struggle with OCD and underscore the importance of seeking help and support.

1.3 THE ROLE OF INTRUSIVE THOUGHTS: UNDERSTANDING THE MENTAL BATTLE

Intrusive thoughts are like unwanted guests that show up at your mind's doorstep, uninvited and persistent. They are distressing, often bizarre thoughts that pop into your head, causing significant anxiety and discomfort. These thoughts can be about anything— violence, harm, taboo subjects, you name it. Imagine sitting in a classroom and suddenly having a vivid thought of yelling out in the middle of a quiet exam. You don't want to do it, but the thought is so intrusive and disturbing that it distracts you from your work.

Everyone experiences intrusive thoughts at some point. It's pretty normal to have an odd or disturbing thought every now and then. But for those with OCD, these thoughts are relentless and far more distressing. The frequency and intensity of these thoughts in OCD make them hard to ignore. For example, a typical person might have a fleeting thought like, "What if I trip and fall during my presentation?" They brush it off and move on. But someone with OCD might obsess over that same thought, imagining every possible way it could go wrong, and feel compelled to perform rituals to prevent it from happening.

So, how can you manage these intrusive thoughts? One helpful strategy is thought-stopping. When an intrusive thought pops up, you can visualize a big red stop sign or say "stop" out loud to interrupt the thought process. Another technique is cognitive restructuring, which involves identifying the irrational thought, challenging its validity, and replacing it with a more balanced thought. For instance, if you think, "I'm going to fail my test because I didn't study enough," you can counter it with, "I've prepared well, and I'll do my best."

Mindful acceptance is another powerful tool. Instead of fighting the intrusive thoughts, observe them without judgment. Picture them as clouds passing by in the sky—acknowledge their presence but let them drift away without engaging. This practice can reduce the power these thoughts have over you.

It's crucial not to engage with or try to suppress these intrusive thoughts. It might seem logical to push them away, but this often makes them stronger and more persistent. This is known as the paradoxical effect; the more you try to avoid or suppress a thought, the more it comes back. Instead, try to observe these thoughts without reacting to them. Realize that a thought is just a thought, not a reflection of reality or your intentions.

One technique to distance yourself from intrusive thoughts is to label them as "just thoughts" and remind yourself that they don't define you. For example, if you have an intrusive thought about hurting someone, tell yourself, "This is just an OCD thought. It doesn't mean I want to do it." This practice helps you separate your identity from the intrusive thoughts and reduces their emotional impact.

Imagine you're watching a scary movie. You know it's just a film and not real life. Similarly, when an intrusive thought pops up, remind yourself it's just a product of your mind, not an actual threat. This perspective can help reduce the anxiety these thoughts cause and make them easier to manage.

In conclusion, intrusive thoughts are a significant part of OCD that can make daily life challenging. However, with strategies like thought-stopping, cognitive restructuring, and mindful acceptance, you can manage these thoughts more effectively. Remember, the goal is not to eliminate intrusive thoughts completely but to reduce their impact and regain control over your mind.

COMPULSIONS AND THEIR CONSEQUENCES: DAILY STRUGGLES AND COPING MECHANISMS

Compulsions are repetitive behaviors or mental acts that you feel driven to perform in response to an obsession. They're not just regular habits or routines but actions you feel you *must* do to reduce the anxiety caused by intrusive thoughts. Think of them as rituals that briefly calm the storm in your mind. Common compulsions include washing your hands excessively, checking locks or appliances multiple times, counting things, or needing to arrange items in a specific order. Mental rituals are different but just as disruptive. These can involve praying, repeating phrases, or mentally reviewing events to ensure nothing bad happens.

The tricky part about compulsions is that they offer short-term relief but reinforce OCD in the long run. Imagine you're feeling anxious because you think your hands are dirty. You wash them, and for a moment, the anxiety fades. But soon enough, the thought returns, often stronger. This is the cycle of obsession and compulsion. The more you give in to the compulsion, the more power the obsession gains. It's a bit like feeding a stray cat—once you start, it keeps coming back, expecting more.

These rituals can be incredibly time-consuming. You might spend hours washing your hands, checking your homework, or arranging your room. This eats into time you could spend on schoolwork, hobbies, or hanging out with friends. It can make you late for school or miss out on social activities. Imagine having to check the door lock ten times before leaving for school; by the time you're done, you're late and stressed out. This disrupts your routine, can lead to family conflicts and affects your school performance.

Socially, compulsions can isolate you. You might avoid situations where you can't perform your rituals, like a friend's sleepover or a school trip. This can lead to feelings of loneliness and make it harder to maintain friendships. Your friends might not understand why you act the way you do, leading to misunderstandings and distance. Family dynamics can also suffer. Parents and siblings might get frustrated with your rituals, not understanding that you *need* to do them to manage your anxiety.

So, how do you break free from this cycle? One effective method is Exposure and Response Prevention (ERP). ERP involves gradually exposing yourself to the source of your anxiety without performing the compulsion. For example, if you feel the need to wash your hands after touching a doorknob, ERP would have you touch the doorknob and then refrain from washing your hands. Over time, this reduces the anxiety associated with the trigger and weakens the compulsion. It's tough, but it works.

Building a supportive routine can also help. Create a schedule that includes time for relaxation, schoolwork, and social activities. This structure can make it easier to manage your day without letting compulsions take over. Distraction techniques are helpful too. Engaging in hobbies or activities you enjoy can divert your mind and reduce the urge to perform compulsions. Whether it's playing a sport, drawing, or playing a musical instrument, finding something you love can be a great way to cope.

Developing a reward system for resisting compulsions can be motivating. Set small, achievable goals and reward yourself for meeting them. Maybe it's treating yourself to your favorite snack or spending extra time on a hobby you enjoy. Positive reinforcement can make a big difference.

Living with OCD is challenging, but understanding your compulsions and how they affect your life is the first step toward managing them. Remember, you're not alone in this. Many people experience these struggles and have found ways to cope effectively. With the right strategies and support, you can reduce the impact of compulsions and lead a more balanced life.

EXTERNALIZING OCD: TAKING BACK CONTROL

∽⯎∾

I magine you're sitting in your favorite spot at the park, trying to enjoy a sunny afternoon. Suddenly, an annoying mosquito starts buzzing around your head, refusing to leave you alone. No matter how hard you try to swat it away, it keeps returning, pestering you until you can't focus on anything else. Now, think of that mosquito as your OCD. Just like that pesky insect, OCD can be persistent and incredibly annoying. But what if you could see it as something separate from yourself, something you could talk back to and eventually manage?

MEET YOUR OCD: PERSONIFYING THE DISORDER

One powerful way to take control of your OCD is by externalizing it, which means seeing it as something outside of yourself rather than an integral part of who you are. This approach can make a huge difference in how you manage your symptoms. By viewing OCD as an external entity, you can start to separate your identity from the intrusive thoughts and compulsive behaviors that it brings. This psychological technique helps reduce self-blame and increases your sense of control over the disorder. When you externalize OCD, you can begin to see it for what it is—a condition that affects you but does not define you.

To start externalizing your OCD, try creating a persona for it. This involves giving your OCD a name and imagining it as a character with specific traits. Think of a name that diminishes its power or makes it easier to confront. It could be something silly like "Mr. Worrywart" or "The Doubter." Naming it can help you see OCD as a separate entity, making it less intimidating. Once you have a name, describe its characteristics. Is it sneaky? Persistent? Annoying? Visualizing these traits can help you understand how OCD operates in your life.

Next, take some time to draw or visualize what your OCD looks like. This might sound a bit odd, but it can be a helpful exercise. Picture your OCD as a cartoon character, a monster, or even a tiny gremlin that sits on your shoulder and whispers in your ear. By giving it a physical form, you can see it as something you can confront and manage. This visualization makes it easier to recognize when OCD is trying to take control, so you can take steps to push back against it.

The benefits of personifying your OCD are significant. For one, it reduces feelings of shame and guilt. When you see OCD as an external force, you can stop blaming yourself for the intrusive thoughts and compulsive behaviors that come with it. This shift in perspective can be incredibly freeing. Additionally, externalizing OCD makes it easier to challenge and confront. It's like dealing with a bully at school—once you see it for what it is, you can stand up to it more confidently. This empowerment can be a game-changer, giving you the motivation and strength to resist OCD's demands.

Here are some exercises to help you meet your OCD and start this process of externalization. First, try writing a letter to your OCD. Address it by the name you've chosen and tell it exactly how you feel about its presence in your life. Be honest and direct. For example, you might write, "Dear Mr. Worrywart, I'm tired of you making me feel anxious all the time. You don't control me, and I'm going to start fighting back." This exercise can help you articulate your feelings and set the stage for taking control.

Another helpful activity is role-playing conversations with your OCD. You can do this alone, with a friend, or even with a family member who understands what you're going through. Pretend you're having a conversation with your OCD, and practice talking back to it. For instance, if your OCD tells you that you need to wash your hands again, respond by saying, "No, I don't need to do that. You're just trying to make me anxious, and I'm not going to listen to you." This practice can build your confidence and make it easier to confront OCD in real-life situations.

Journaling about OCD's influence on your daily life is another effective tool. Keep a journal where you document instances when your OCD tries to take over. Describe what happened, how you felt, and how you responded. Reflect on these experiences and think about what you can do differently next time. This reflection can help you identify patterns in your OCD behavior and develop strategies to manage it more effectively.

By externalizing your OCD and seeing it as a separate entity, you can start to regain control over your life. This approach helps reduce the power OCD has over you and makes it easier to challenge and confront. Remember, OCD is just a part of your life; it doesn't define who you are. With the right tools and mindset, you can take control and live a life that OCD does not dominate.

TALKING BACK TO OCD: TECHNIQUES FOR GAINING CONTROL

Imagine you're at a party, and this annoying guest keeps following you around, saying things to make you feel bad. Ignoring them doesn't seem to work; they just get louder and more persistent. What if you could stand up to them and tell them to back off? That's kind of what you need to do with OCD. Ignoring OCD doesn't work because it thrives on your inaction and fear. The more you try to avoid it, the stronger it becomes. Actively confronting OCD, on the other hand, helps you reclaim control. By taking an assertive stance, you show OCD that you're not going to let it push you around anymore. This shift in attitude can weaken the hold OCD has on you, making it easier to manage your symptoms.

One effective way to talk back to OCD is to use assertive language. When an intrusive thought pops up, challenge it directly. For example, if you get a thought like, "I need to wash my hands again, or I'll get sick," respond with, "I don't have to listen to you, OCD. You're just trying to make me anxious." This kind of self-talk can help reduce the power of intrusive thoughts and make them easier to ignore. Developing a mantra or affirmation can also be helpful. Choose a phrase that resonates with you and repeat it whenever OCD tries to take over. Something like, "I am stronger than my OCD" or "These thoughts don't control me" can serve as a mental shield against the intrusive ideas.

To get a better sense of how to talk back to OCD, let's look at some real-life examples and scripts. Imagine you have contamination fears and constantly feel the need to wash your hands. When the thought "I need to wash my hands now" comes up, you can counter it with, "No, I don't need to wash my hands. OCD, you're lying to me." If you struggle with intrusive thoughts about harm, you might say, "These thoughts are just OCD. They don't reflect who I am or what I want." Practicing these scripts can make it easier to confront OCD in the moment.

Consistent practice is key to making these techniques effective. It's like building a muscle—the more you use it, the stronger it gets. Set aside time each day for "talk back" exercises. You can do this in front of a mirror, write it down, or even practice with a trusted friend or family member. Tracking your progress in a journal can also be incredibly helpful. Note down the instances when you successfully talked back to OCD and how you felt afterward. This can provide a sense of accomplishment and show you how far you've come, even on days when it feels like you're not making progress. Reward yourself for successful confrontations. It doesn't have to be anything big—maybe treat yourself to a favorite snack or take some time to do an activity you enjoy. Positive reinforcement can make the process less daunting and more rewarding.

Imagine you're dealing with an intrusive thought while sitting in class. The thought is telling you that you need to tap your desk ten times or something bad will happen. Instead of giving in, you could say to yourself, "This is just my OCD talking. Tapping my desk won't change anything." Then, focus on your breathing or redirect your attention to the lesson. The more you practice this, the easier it becomes to resist the urge and focus on what's important.

Talking back to OCD is about reclaiming your voice and your power. It's about standing up to that annoying guest at the party and telling them they're not welcome. It's about recognizing that OCD is a bully that thrives on your fear and inaction. By confronting it head-on, you can start to weaken its hold on you and regain control of your life. Keep practicing, stay consistent, and remember that every small victory is a step toward a life less dominated by OCD.

THE POWER OF NAMING: HOW GIVING OCD A NAME CAN HELP

Imagine having a bully who constantly follows you around, whispering mean things in your ear. This bully tells you that you need to wash your hands again and check the locks one more time, or else something terrible will happen. What if you could give this bully a name, making it easier to recognize and stand up to it? Naming your OCD can be a powerful way to create a clear distinction between yourself and the disorder. It helps you see OCD as something separate from who you are, making it feel more manageable and less overwhelming.

When you give your OCD a name, you take the first step in taking back control. It's like labeling a folder on your computer—once it has a name, you know exactly what it contains and can deal with it more effectively. The psychological impact of this simple act can be profound. It helps you externalize the disorder, reducing the feelings of shame and guilt that often come with it. You begin to see OCD as an external force that you can confront rather than an inseparable part of your identity.

Choosing a name for your OCD can be a fun and creative process. Think of names that resonate with you and diminish OCD's power. For example, you could call it "Mr. Worrywart" or "The Doubter." Silly or diminutive names can make the disorder seem less intimidating and easier to handle. The goal is to come up with a name that makes you feel empowered and ready to take on the challenge. Ask your friends or family for suggestions, or brainstorm on your own until you find a name that feels right.

Let's look at some stories from other teens who have successfully named their OCD. Take Emma, for example. Emma struggled with intrusive thoughts about germs and contamination. She decided to call her OCD "The Bully," recognizing that it was trying to intimidate her into performing rituals. Naming it helped her see the disorder as a separate entity that she could stand up to. Whenever "The Bully" tried to take over, Emma would remind herself that she was stronger and didn't have to give in.

Jake had a different experience. He dealt with intrusive thoughts about harming others, which made him feel guilty and scared. Jake decided to name his OCD "The Doubter" because it always made him doubt his intentions and actions. By giving it a name, Jake could distance himself from the intrusive thoughts and see them for what they were—symptoms of his disorder, not reflections of his true self. This shift in perspective helped Jake gain the confidence to challenge and resist his OCD.

If you're ready to name your OCD, here are some exercises to help you get started. Begin with a brainstorming session. Sit down with a notebook and jot down any names that come to mind. Don't overthink it—just let your creativity flow. You can do this alone or with the help of friends and family. Once you have a list of potential names, choose the one that resonates most with you.

Next, try drawing or crafting a visual representation of your named OCD. This can be as simple or elaborate as you like. You might draw a cartoon character, create a collage, or even build a small model. The goal is to give your OCD a tangible form that you can see and recognize. This visualization can make it easier to confront and challenge the disorder.

Writing about how naming your OCD changes your perspective can also be a helpful exercise. Take some time to reflect on how you feel now that your OCD has a name. Does it seem less intimidating? Do you feel more in control? Write down your thoughts and feelings in a journal. This reflection can reinforce the benefits of externalizing your OCD and help you stay motivated in your efforts to manage it.

By naming your OCD, you take a significant step in reclaiming your power and control. This simple act can make the disorder feel more manageable and less overwhelming, giving you the confidence to stand up to it. So go ahead, give your OCD a name, and start seeing it for what it is—a challenge you can overcome, not a defining part of who you are.

CREATING YOUR OCD BATTLE PLAN: PRACTICAL STRATEGIES FOR DAILY LIFE

When it comes to managing OCD, having a clear, personalized battle plan can make all the difference. Think of your plan as a roadmap that guides you through the ups and downs of dealing with OCD. The first step is to identify your specific OCD triggers and responses. Start by keeping a journal where you note down situations that trigger your obsessions and the compulsions that follow. For instance, you might notice that your anxiety spikes when you touch doorknobs, leading you to wash your hands repeatedly. Recognizing these patterns helps you understand where to focus your efforts.

Next, set clear, achievable goals. These goals should be specific and attainable so you don't feel overwhelmed. For example, if you wash your hands 20 times a day, aim to reduce it to 18 times for the first week. Gradually lower the number as you gain confidence. Setting small, manageable goals makes the process less intimidating and allows you to celebrate your progress along the way. Break down each goal into smaller steps and tackle them one at a time.

Now, let's dive into some practical, actionable strategies for daily management. One effective technique is scheduling "worry time." Allocate a specific time each day, say 15-20 minutes, to focus on your worries and obsessions. During this period, allow yourself to think about your intrusive thoughts, but only during this set time. Outside of these minutes, remind yourself that you'll deal with the worries later. This method helps limit OCD's interference in your daily activities and gives you a sense of control.

Creating a reward system for resisting compulsions can be highly motivating. For instance, if you manage to reduce a compulsion or resist it altogether, reward yourself with something you enjoy—a favorite snack, a break to watch a funny video, or extra time playing a game. Positive reinforcement can make the challenging process of resisting compulsions more rewarding and less daunting.

Developing a daily routine that incorporates coping strategies is also crucial. Start by structuring your day to include regular breaks for relaxation and mindfulness exercises. Plan your study or work sessions with short intervals to practice deep breathing or quick stretches. This routine not only helps manage OCD symptoms but also promotes overall well-being. Consistency is key, so try to stick to your routine as much as possible, even on days when OCD feels particularly overwhelming.

To help you get started, here are some templates and examples. Use daily and weekly planners to organize your tasks and coping strategies. For example, your daily planner could include time for schoolwork, relaxation breaks, and "worry time." Progress tracking charts can be helpful to visualize your achievements. Create a chart where you can mark off each time you successfully resist a compulsion or complete a goal. Seeing your progress in a tangible way can boost your motivation and confidence.

Involving your family in your battle plan can provide additional support and encouragement. Hold regular family meetings to review and adjust your plan as needed. Your parents or siblings can play a crucial role in providing accountability and encouragement. For example, they can remind you to stick to your routine or celebrate your achievements with you. Creating a supportive home environment is essential. Encourage your family to learn about OCD and understand your specific triggers and challenges. This knowledge can help them offer better support and avoid unintentional actions that might exacerbate your symptoms.

Your battle plan should be a living document, constantly evolving as you make progress and face new challenges. Keep it flexible and adapt it to fit your changing needs. With a clear plan in place, you'll feel more equipped to tackle OCD head-on and regain control over your life.

As we wrap up this chapter, remember that developing your personalized OCD battle plan is a critical step in managing the disorder. By identifying your triggers, setting achievable goals, and incorporating practical strategies into your daily life, you can reduce the power OCD has over you. With the support of your family and the right tools in your arsenal, you're ready to take on the challenges ahead.

PROVEN THERAPEUTIC TECHNIQUES: CBT, DBT, AND ACT

I magine you're sitting at your desk, staring at your homework, but unable to start because your mind keeps telling you that if you don't get it perfect, something bad will happen. You know it's irrational, but the anxiety is so overwhelming that you feel paralyzed. This is where Cognitive Behavioral Therapy (CBT) comes in. It's a proven technique that helps you change these negative thought patterns and behaviors, making it easier to manage your OCD.

COGNITIVE BEHAVIORAL THERAPY (CBT): REWIRING YOUR BRAIN

CBT is a type of therapy focused on changing the way you think and behave. It's based on the idea that our thoughts, feelings, and behaviors are all interconnected. When you have a negative thought, it can lead to negative emotions, which then result in unhelpful behaviors. For example, if you think, "If I don't wash my hands again, I'll get sick," this thought creates anxiety (a negative feeling), which then drives you to wash your hands repeatedly (an unhelpful behavior). CBT aims to break this cycle by helping you identify and challenge these negative thoughts, ultimately leading to healthier behaviors and emotions.

One of the first steps in CBT is recognizing cognitive distortions. These irrational thoughts skew your perception of reality, making you feel worse. Common distortions include black-and-white thinking ("If I fail this test, I'm a complete failure"), catastrophizing ("If I don't check the door, someone will break in and harm my family"), and overgeneralization ("I made a mistake, so I must be a terrible person"). By learning to spot these distortions, you can start to challenge and change them.

Cognitive restructuring is a core part of CBT. This process involves identifying your automatic negative thoughts and learning to reframe them in a more positive or realistic way. Let's say you have the thought, "I'm a failure because I didn't get an A on my test." This thought can be challenged by asking yourself questions like, "Is it true that one test grade defines my entire worth?" and "What evidence do I have that I'm actually a failure?" By questioning these negative thoughts, you can start to reframe them. Instead of thinking, "I'm a failure," reframe it to, "I'm learning and improving, and one grade doesn't define me."

Another crucial component of CBT for OCD is Exposure and Response Prevention (ERP). ERP involves gradually exposing yourself to the situations that trigger your obsessions while preventing the compulsive response. The goal is to reduce the anxiety associated with the trigger and weaken the compulsion over time. For example, if touching doorknobs triggers your fear of contamination, ERP would have you touch doorknobs without washing your hands afterward. Initially, this exposure will cause anxiety, but with repeated practice, the anxiety will decrease, and the compulsion will weaken.

The steps involved in ERP start with creating a fear hierarchy. List the situations that trigger your OCD from least to most anxiety-provoking. Then, begin with the least anxiety-inducing situation and gradually work your way up. For instance, if your fear hierarchy includes touching a book that someone else has touched, start there before moving on to more challenging tasks like shaking hands or using public restrooms. The key is to expose yourself gradually and consistently, allowing the anxiety to decrease naturally over time.

To practice these CBT techniques, you'll need some practical tools. Thought record worksheets can help you track and challenge your negative thoughts. Write down the situation that triggered the thought, the thought itself, and the emotion you felt, and then challenge the thought with questions like, "What evidence do I have for and against this thought?" and "Is there another way to look at this situation?" This exercise helps you see the irrationality of your thoughts and find more balanced perspectives.

Fear hierarchy charts are essential for ERP. Create a list of situations that trigger your OCD and rank them from least to most anxiety-provoking. Start with the least challenging situation and work your way up. Record your progress and note any changes in your anxiety levels. This visual representation can make the process less overwhelming and more manageable.

Daily CBT practice logs are also beneficial. Keep a journal where you document your daily experiences, the thoughts and feelings that arise, and how you respond to them. This practice helps you stay consistent and track your progress over time. It also provides a sense of accomplishment as you see how far you've come in managing your OCD.

One effective exercise is the thought record worksheet. Suppose you catch yourself thinking, "I'll never get better at this." Write it down and challenge it. Ask yourself, "Is this thought based on facts or feelings?" and "What evidence do I have that contradicts this thought?" Perhaps you've made small improvements already, like reducing the time spent on compulsions. Reframe the thought to, "I am making progress, even if it's slow."

Creating a fear hierarchy chart can help with ERP. List your triggers from least to most anxiety-inducing. For example, touching a door-knob might be less scary than using a public restroom. Start with the doorknob and expose yourself to it without performing the compulsion. Gradually move up your list, giving yourself time to adapt at each step.

By incorporating these CBT techniques into your daily life, you can start to rewire your brain, change negative thought patterns, and reduce compulsive behaviors. Remember, it takes time and practice, but with persistence, you can make significant progress.

DIALECTICAL BEHAVIOR THERAPY (DBT): BALANCING EMOTIONS AND ACTIONS

Dialectical Behavior Therapy, or DBT, is a type of therapy that combines cognitive-behavioral techniques with mindfulness to help you manage your emotions and actions more effectively. Unlike traditional CBT, DBT places a strong emphasis on balancing accep-tance and change. This means recognizing and accepting your current emotions and thoughts while also working toward positive change. The core principles of DBT include mindfulness, distress tolerance, emotion regulation, and interpersonal effectiveness. These principles work together to help you stay grounded, handle stress, manage your emotions, and improve your relationships.

Mindfulness is all about staying present and fully aware of your thoughts and emotions without judgment. This practice can be incredibly helpful in reducing OCD symptoms by allowing you to observe your intrusive thoughts without reacting to them. One simple mindfulness exercise is the body scan. Start by sitting or lying down in a comfortable position. Close your eyes and take a few deep breaths. Slowly bring your attention to different parts of your body, starting from your toes and working your way up to your head. Notice any sensations, tension, or discomfort, and just observe them without trying to change anything. Another effective technique is mindful breathing. Focus on your breath as it enters and leaves your body. When your mind starts to wander, gently bring it back to your breath. Practicing these exercises regularly can help you become more aware of your thoughts and reduce the impact of intrusive thoughts by observing them without judgment.

Distress tolerance skills are crucial for managing intense emotions without resorting to compulsions. These skills help you tolerate and survive crises without making things worse. One set of distress tolerance skills is known as "TIPP" – Temperature, Intense Exercise, Paced Breathing, and Progressive Relaxation. When you're feeling overwhelmed, try changing your body temperature by holding a cold pack or splashing cold water on your face. This can help calm your nervous system. Intense exercise, like running or doing jumping jacks, can also release built-up energy and reduce anxiety. Paced breathing involves taking slow, deep breaths to help calm your mind and body. Lastly, progressive relaxation involves tensing and then relaxing different muscle groups in your body, which can help release physical tension and reduce stress. By practicing these skills, you can manage your emotions more effectively and reduce the urge to engage in compulsive behaviors.

Emotion regulation strategies are designed to help you understand and manage your emotions more effectively. One important aspect of emotion regulation is identifying and labeling your emotions. When you're feeling overwhelmed, take a moment to pause and ask yourself, "What am I feeling right now?" Try to name the emotion as accurately as possible, whether it's anxiety, sadness, frustration, or something else. Once you've identified the emotion, you can work on changing your emotional response. One technique for doing this is the opposite action technique. This involves doing the opposite of what your emotion is urging you to do. For example, if you're feeling the urge to isolate yourself because you're anxious, try reaching out to a friend or family member instead. This can help break the cycle of negative emotions and lead to more positive outcomes.

Interpersonal effectiveness is another critical component of DBT. This involves learning how to communicate more effectively and build healthier relationships. One important skill in this area is assertiveness, which means expressing your needs and feelings in a clear, respectful way. For example, if you feel overwhelmed by a friend's behavior, you might say, "I feel really stressed when you talk about that topic. Can we change the subject?" By practicing assertiveness, you can improve your relationships and reduce the stress that can trigger OCD symptoms.

Practicing mindfulness and learning to tolerate distress are powerful tools in managing OCD. By staying present and aware of your thoughts and emotions without judgment, you can reduce the impact of intrusive thoughts. Distress tolerance skills help you manage intense emotions without resorting to compulsions, while emotion regulation strategies enable you to understand and change your emotional responses. Interpersonal effectiveness skills improve your relationships and reduce stress, further helping you manage OCD.

Through DBT, you can find a balance between accepting your current experiences and working toward positive change.

ACCEPTANCE AND COMMITMENT THERAPY (ACT): EMBRACING YOUR THOUGHTS

Imagine sitting in class, and your mind keeps bombarding you with intrusive thoughts. No matter how hard you try to push them away, they keep coming back, stronger and more persistent. Acceptance and Commitment Therapy (ACT) offers a different approach. Instead of fighting these thoughts, ACT teaches you to accept them while committing to actions that align with your values. The idea is to embrace your thoughts and feelings without letting them control your actions.

ACT revolves around six core processes that help you develop psychological flexibility, which is the ability to adapt to different situations with an open mind. These processes are acceptance, cognitive defusion, being present, self as context, values, and committed action. Acceptance involves allowing your thoughts and feelings to exist without trying to change them. Cognitive defusion helps you see thoughts as just thoughts, not facts. Being present means staying focused on the here and now. Self as context is about seeing yourself as more than just your thoughts and feelings. Values are what truly matter to you, and committed action is about taking steps that align with those values.

Learning to accept your thoughts and feelings can be challenging, but it's a crucial part of ACT. Mindfulness and non-judgmental observation are key techniques for acceptance. When an intrusive thought pops up, instead of trying to push it away, acknowledge it. You might say to yourself, "I notice that I'm having a thought about contamination." This simple act of acknowledgment can reduce the thought's power over you. Cognitive defusion exercises further help by creating distance between you and your thoughts. One effective exercise is the "Leaves on a stream" visualization. Imagine sitting by a stream and placing each intrusive thought on a leaf, letting it float away. This exercise helps you see thoughts as external objects that come and go, rather than defining you.

Identifying your values is another important aspect of ACT. Values are like a compass that guides your actions and decisions. Take some time to reflect on what truly matters to you. Ask yourself questions like, "What kind of person do I want to be?" and "What do I want to stand for?" Exercises like the values clarification worksheet can help you pinpoint your core values. Write down your top values and think about how they can guide your daily actions. For example, if kindness is a core value, consider ways you can incorporate acts of kindness into your routine, even when OCD tries to interfere.

Once you've identified your values, it's time to take committed action. This means setting goals that align with your values and taking concrete steps to achieve them. Start by setting small, achievable goals. For instance, if you value education but OCD makes it hard to focus on homework, set a goal to work on an assignment for just 10 minutes without giving in to compulsions. Gradually increase the time as you build confidence. Overcoming barriers to committed action is also essential. You might face obstacles like fear of failure or discomfort from intrusive thoughts. Recognize these barriers and develop strategies to overcome them, such as breaking tasks into smaller steps or using mindfulness to stay focused.

Creating an action plan can make the process more manageable. Write down your values-based goals and outline the steps needed to achieve them. For example, if pursuing a personal passion like playing an instrument is important to you, create a plan that includes daily practice sessions, finding a mentor, and setting performance goals. This structured approach helps you stay on track and provides a sense of accomplishment as you make progress.

ACT encourages you to embrace your thoughts and feelings without letting them dictate your actions. By accepting your inner experiences and committing to actions that align with your values, you can lead a more fulfilling and meaningful life. Remember, it's not about eliminating intrusive thoughts but learning to live with them in a way that doesn't hinder your growth and happiness.

THE TRIPLE-A RESPONSE®: A UNIQUE APPROACH TO MANAGING OCD

Managing OCD can feel like an uphill battle, but the Triple-A Response® offers a structured, effective method to tackle those relentless thoughts and behaviors. This approach involves three core components: Awareness, Acceptance, and Action. By integrating these elements into your daily life, you can start to regain control over your OCD symptoms and create a more balanced, fulfilling existence.

First, let's talk about Awareness. Becoming aware of your OCD patterns is crucial for managing the disorder effectively. Awareness involves recognizing the triggers and symptoms that set off your obsessive thoughts and compulsive behaviors. One way to increase self-awareness is through journaling. Keeping a daily log of your thoughts, feelings, and behaviors can help you identify patterns and triggers. For instance, you might notice that your anxiety spikes when you're under academic pressure, leading to an increase in compulsive behaviors like checking or washing. Mindfulness exercises are another excellent tool for boosting self-awareness. By practicing mindfulness, you learn to observe your thoughts and feelings without getting caught up in them. This can help you recognize when OCD is trying to take control, allowing you to intervene more effectively. Imagine keeping a daily awareness log where you jot down each instance of OCD behavior, noting the trigger and your emotional response. This simple practice can provide invaluable insights into your OCD patterns, making it easier to manage them.

Next up is Acceptance. This step involves acknowledging your thoughts and feelings without judgment or resistance. It might sound counterintuitive, but accepting your intrusive thoughts can actually reduce their power over you. Techniques for practicing acceptance include mindfulness and self-compassion exercises. Mindfulness teaches you to observe your thoughts and feelings without reacting to them. For example, if you have an intrusive thought about contamination, instead of trying to push it away, you might say to yourself, "I notice that I'm having a thought about germs." This non-judgmental observation can help you detach from the thought and reduce its impact. Another useful technique is self-compassion. When you're struggling with OCD, it's easy to be hard on yourself. Practicing self-compassion involves treating yourself with the same kindness and understanding that you would offer to a friend. One way to do this is through self-compassion exercises. For instance, when you're feeling overwhelmed by OCD, take a moment to acknowledge your struggle and offer yourself some words of kindness. You might say, "I'm having a hard time right now, but that's okay. I'm doing my best, and that's enough."

The final component of the Triple-A Response® is Action. This step involves taking proactive measures to manage your OCD symptoms. Developing an action plan can provide a clear roadmap for addressing your specific challenges. One effective strategy is to incorporate Exposure and Response Prevention (ERP) into your action plan. ERP involves gradually exposing yourself to your OCD triggers without performing the compulsive behavior. For example, if you have a fear of contamination, your action plan might include tasks like touching a doorknob without washing your hands afterward. Start with less anxiety-provoking tasks and gradually work your way up. Another useful technique is to create a daily action plan that outlines specific goals and coping strategies. For instance, your action plan might include tasks like practicing mindfulness for 10 minutes each morning, using a grounding technique when you feel anxious, and rewarding yourself for resisting compulsions. By taking these proactive steps, you can start to regain control over your OCD and improve your overall well-being.

As we wrap up this chapter on the Triple-A Response®, remember that Awareness, Acceptance, and Action are your tools for managing OCD. By integrating these components into your daily life, you can reduce the power of intrusive thoughts and compulsive behaviors. Keep practicing, stay consistent, and know that every small step brings you closer to a life less dominated by OCD. Next, we'll explore how mindfulness and meditation can further support your journey to peace and freedom.

MINDFULNESS AND MEDITATION PRACTICES

$\approx$

Picture this: you're sitting in your room, trying to study for an upcoming test. Your mind is racing with thoughts about whether you locked the front door, if you washed your hands enough times, or if you'll fail the test because you can't focus. These thoughts are like a storm, and you're caught in the middle, unable to find peace. What if I told you there's a way to calm this storm, to find a sense of peace right in the middle of the chaos? That's where mindfulness comes in.

MINDFULNESS 101: STAYING PRESENT AMIDST THE CHAOS

Mindfulness is the practice of staying present and fully engaging with the current moment. It's about paying attention to what's happening right now without getting lost in thoughts about the past or worries about the future. Imagine being able to focus on your breath, notice the sensation of your feet touching the ground, or simply enjoy the sound of birds outside your window. This is mindfulness. It helps you anchor yourself in the present, providing a break from the relentless stream of thoughts that often comes with OCD.

The benefits of mindfulness for mental health are well-documented. Research shows that practicing mindfulness can reduce anxiety, improve mood, and even help manage symptoms of OCD. It helps you observe your thoughts and feelings without judgment, giving you the space to respond to them in a more balanced way. Instead of reacting to every intrusive thought, mindfulness teaches you to acknowledge these thoughts and let them pass, reducing their impact on your life. By focusing on the present moment, you can break free from the cycle of obsessions and compulsions, finding a sense of calm amidst the storm.

So, how do you actually practice mindfulness? It starts with simple, actionable steps. The first step is to focus on the present moment. This means paying attention to what you're doing right now, whether it's eating, walking, or even just breathing. Notice the details of your experience—the taste of your food, the feeling of the ground under your feet, or the rhythm of your breath. The goal is to fully engage with the present moment, letting go of thoughts about the past or future.

Another key aspect of mindfulness is observing your thoughts and emotions without judgment. When an intrusive thought pops up, don't try to push it away or judge yourself for having it. Instead, acknowledge it and let it pass. You might say to yourself, "I notice that I'm having a thought about germs," and then gently bring your focus back to the present moment. This non-judgmental observation helps reduce the power of intrusive thoughts, making them easier to manage.

Techniques for grounding yourself can also be incredibly helpful. One effective technique is to notice your five senses. Take a moment to identify five things you can see, four things you can touch, three things you can hear, two things you can smell, and one thing you can taste. This exercise helps anchor you in the present moment, providing a break from the constant stream of thoughts. Another grounding technique is to focus on the feeling of your feet touching the ground. Notice the sensation of the ground beneath your feet, the pressure, and the texture. This simple act of paying attention to your body can help bring you back to the present moment.

The science behind mindfulness supports its effectiveness in reducing anxiety and stress. Studies have shown that mindfulness practices can lead to significant reductions in OCD symptoms. For example, a 2013 study found that mindfulness reduced the urge to neutralize thoughts with compulsions. Another study conducted in 2012 showed that an 8-week mindfulness-based group therapy program led to reduced OCD symptoms in participants. The brain also changes with mindfulness practice. Research indicates that mindfulness can increase the thickness of the prefrontal cortex, the part of the brain responsible for decision-making and emotional regulation. It can also reduce the size of the amygdala, the brain's fear center, leading to lower levels of anxiety.

Let's try a simple mindfulness exercise to get you started. This is called a body scan exercise, and it's a great way to practice mindfulness and relax your body. Find a quiet place where you won't be disturbed. Sit or lie down in a comfortable position. Close your eyes and take a few deep breaths. Start by focusing on your toes. Notice any sensations you feel—tingling, warmth, or even numbness. Slowly move your attention up to your feet, ankles, and legs, paying attention to any sensations you experience. Continue this process, moving up through your body, focusing on each part—your hips, stomach, chest, arms, and finally, your head. As you scan each part of your body, observe any sensations without judgment. Just notice them and then move on to the next part. This exercise helps you become more aware of your body and stay present in the moment.

Practicing mindfulness daily can make a big difference in managing OCD symptoms. Start with just a few minutes each day and gradually increase the time as you become more comfortable with the practice. The more you practice, the easier it becomes to stay present and reduce the impact of intrusive thoughts. Remember, mindfulness is a skill that takes time to develop, so be patient with yourself and keep practicing.

GUIDED MEDITATION FOR OCD: STEP-BY-STEP PRACTICES

Guided meditation can be a game-changer, especially if you're new to the practice. Think of it as having a personal coach in your ear, guiding you through each step. This structure can be incredibly beneficial, offering a safe space to explore meditation without feeling lost or unsure. Guided meditations help reduce intrusive thoughts and anxiety by directing your focus and providing a sense of calm. They also promote relaxation and better emotional regulation, making it easier to deal with the ups and downs that come with OCD.

Let's start with setting up a comfortable space. Find a quiet spot where you won't be disturbed. This could be your room, a cozy corner in your house, or even a peaceful spot outside. Make sure it's a place where you feel safe and relaxed. Sit or lie down in a comfortable position. You might want to use a cushion or blanket to make yourself more comfortable. The goal is to create a space where you can fully relax and focus on the meditation.

Begin by focusing on your breath. Close your eyes and take a few deep breaths. Inhale slowly through your nose, allowing your belly to rise, and then exhale through your mouth. As you continue to breathe deeply, let go of any tension in your body. Bring your attention to the sensation of your breath entering and leaving your body. Notice how your chest and belly move with each breath. If your mind starts to wander, gently bring your focus back to your breath. This simple act of focusing on your breath can help anchor you in the present moment and reduce the impact of intrusive thoughts.

Visualization techniques can also create a sense of calm. Imagine a peaceful scene that makes you feel relaxed. This could be a beach with gentle waves, a quiet forest with birds singing, or a cozy room with a warm fire. Picture yourself in this place, noticing the details —the sound of the waves, the smell of the forest, or the warmth of the fire. Allow yourself to fully immerse in this scene, letting go of any stress or anxiety. Visualization can help shift your focus away from intrusive thoughts and create a sense of peace and relaxation.

Now, let's explore specific guided meditations tailored to OCD symptoms. For intrusive thoughts, imagine these thoughts as clouds passing in the sky. When an intrusive thought pops up, visualize it as a cloud drifting by. Acknowledge the thought without judgment and let it pass, just like a cloud in the sky. This visualization helps you see intrusive thoughts as temporary and not something you need to engage with. For compulsive urges, try visualizing a calm wave washing over the urge. Imagine the urge as a wave building up, and then visualize a bigger, calmer wave washing over it, reducing its intensity. This technique can help you manage the urge without giving in to it.

To support your meditation practice, there are several resources available. Meditation apps like Headspace and Calm offer a variety of guided meditations that you can try. These apps provide structured sessions that are easy to follow, making them perfect for beginners. You can also find free online guided meditations on websites like YouTube or the International OCD Foundation's website. Look for meditations specifically designed for OCD to get the most benefit. Creating a personal meditation playlist can also be helpful. Compile your favorite guided meditations into a playlist that you can easily access whenever you need a moment of calm. This makes it convenient to practice meditation regularly, even on busy days.

Guided meditation offers a structured, supportive way to explore mindfulness and relaxation. By setting up a comfortable space, focusing on your breath, and using visualization techniques, you can create a sense of calm and reduce the impact of intrusive thoughts and compulsive urges. With the help of resources like meditation apps and online guided meditations, you can build a consistent practice that supports your mental and emotional well-being.

MINDFUL BREATHING: TECHNIQUES TO CALM YOUR MIND

Ever noticed how your breath changes when you're stressed? It becomes shallow, rapid, almost like you can't catch it. That's because your breath is closely tied to your nervous system. When you're anxious, your body goes into fight-or-flight mode, making your breathing fast and shallow. But you can flip the switch by focusing on your breath. Deep, mindful breathing sends signals to your brain that it's okay to relax, calming your nervous system and reducing anxiety. It's like having a built-in stress-relief button that you can press anytime.

Deep, mindful breathing has tons of benefits for stress reduction. When you breathe deeply, you activate the parasympathetic nervous system, which is responsible for rest and relaxation. This helps lower your heart rate, reduce blood pressure, and calm your mind. It's a simple, natural way to ease the tension that builds up from dealing with OCD. Plus, it's something you can do anywhere, anytime. Whether you're sitting in class, lying in bed, or waiting for the bus, a few minutes of deep breathing can make a huge difference.

Let's dive into some basic breathing exercises you can try. One of the simplest and most effective techniques is diaphragmatic breathing, also known as belly breathing. Start by sitting or lying down in a comfortable position. Place one hand on your belly and the other on your chest. Take a slow, deep breath in through your nose, allowing your belly to rise as it fills with air. The hand on your belly should move more than the one on your chest. Exhale slowly through your mouth, letting your belly fall. Feel the rise and fall of your belly with each breath. This helps ensure you're breathing deeply, not just from your chest, which can help calm your mind and body.

Another great technique is the 4-7-8 breathing method. This works wonders for reducing anxiety and helping you relax. Start by finding a quiet spot where you can sit comfortably. Close your eyes and take a deep breath in through your nose for a count of four. Hold your breath for a count of seven. Then, exhale completely through your mouth for a count of eight. Repeat this cycle a few times. The longer exhale helps expel more carbon dioxide, which can promote relaxation. This technique can be especially helpful before bed or during moments of high stress.

For those who want to deepen their practice, advanced breathing techniques offer even more benefits. Alternate nostril breathing is a technique that balances the body and mind. Sit comfortably and use your right thumb to close your right nostril. Inhale deeply through your left nostril. Close your left nostril with your ring finger, and then release your right nostril. Exhale through your right nostril. Inhale through your right nostril, close it with your thumb, and exhale through your left nostril. This completes one cycle. Repeat several cycles, focusing on the flow of breath through each nostril.

Box breathing, also known as square breathing, is another advanced technique. It's used by Navy SEALs to stay calm under pressure, and it's great for managing anxiety. Sit comfortably and close your eyes. Inhale through your nose for a count of four. Hold your breath for a count of four. Exhale through your mouth for a count of four. Hold your breath again for a count of four. Repeat this cycle for a few minutes. The steady rhythm of box breathing can help ground you and bring a sense of calm.

Consistency is key to reaping the benefits of mindful breathing. Try to incorporate these exercises into your daily routine. Maybe start your day with a few minutes of diaphragmatic breathing, or use the 4-7-8 technique before bed to help you unwind. Practice during stressful moments too. If you're feeling overwhelmed at school, take a few deep breaths to center yourself. Creating a calming environment can make practice more effective. Find a quiet spot, dim the lights, and maybe play some soothing music. The more you practice, the easier it becomes to use these techniques whenever you need a moment of calm.

4.4 DAILY MINDFULNESS ROUTINES: INTEGRATING PRACTICES INTO YOUR LIFE

Imagine waking up every day with a sense of calm and clarity. Consistent mindfulness practice can help you achieve that. Building regular mindfulness routines can strengthen your resilience and gradually reduce OCD symptoms. Think of mindfulness as a workout for your mind. Just like regular physical exercise keeps your body fit, consistent mindfulness practice keeps your mind sharp and balanced. Over time, this can lead to significant improvements in your mental health and overall well-being. You'll find that the more you practice, the easier it becomes to handle intrusive thoughts and compulsive behaviors.

Creating a daily mindfulness routine doesn't have to be complicated. Start with a morning mindfulness practice. As soon as you wake up, take five minutes to sit quietly and focus on your breath. This simple act can set a calm tone for the rest of your day. You could also incorporate a brief body scan, checking in with how each part of your body feels. This helps you start the day grounded and aware, making it easier to stay present and focused. Another great routine is an evening reflection practice. Before bed, spend a few minutes journaling about your day's mindfulness moments. Write down any times you felt particularly present or any challenges you faced. Reflecting on these moments can help reinforce your practice and provide insights into how mindfulness is impacting your life.

Mindfulness isn't limited to sitting meditation. You can integrate it into everyday activities, turning ordinary moments into opportunities for practice. Take mindful eating, for example. Instead of rushing through meals, take the time to really taste and savor each bite. Notice the texture, flavor, and aroma of your food. This not only enhances your enjoyment but also helps you stay present.

Another activity is mindful walking. As you walk, pay attention to each step, the feel of the ground under your feet, and the rhythm of your movements. This can be especially calming and is a great way to incorporate mindfulness into your daily routine. Mindful listening is another powerful practice. When you're in a conversation, fully focus on the person speaking. Notice their words, tone, and body language. This improves your listening skills and helps you stay engaged and present.

It's important to remember that mindfulness routines should be flexible and tailored to fit your lifestyle. What works for one person might not work for another, so don't be afraid to experiment and find what resonates with you. If you're a morning person, you might enjoy starting your day with mindfulness. If you're more of a night owl, an evening practice might suit you better. The key is to find a routine that feels natural and sustainable. You might combine different practices, like starting the day with a short meditation and ending it with mindful journaling. Or you might prefer integrating mindfulness into activities you already do, like eating or walking. The goal is to create a routine that supports your mental health and fits seamlessly into your life.

Here are some tips to help you adapt your mindfulness practice to your lifestyle. Start small. You don't need to dedicate hours to mindfulness each day. Even a few minutes can make a big difference. Be consistent. Try to practice at the same time each day to create a habit. Find what works for you. Experiment with different practices and routines until you find what feels right. Combine practices. Mix and match different mindfulness activities to keep things interesting and engaging. Be patient with yourself. Mindfulness is a skill that takes time to develop, so don't get discouraged if you find it challenging at first.

By integrating mindfulness into your daily life, you can build resilience, reduce OCD symptoms, and enhance your overall well-being. Remember, the goal is to stay present and fully engage with each moment, whether you're meditating, eating, walking, or listening. With regular practice, mindfulness can become a natural and supportive part of your daily routine, helping you navigate the challenges of OCD with greater ease and confidence.

In the next chapter, we'll explore the role of setting SMART goals in managing OCD, offering practical strategies to help you achieve your objectives and track your progress.

SETTING SMART GOALS

Imagine you're on a road trip, but you don't have a map or any idea where you're going. You end up driving around aimlessly, feeling frustrated and lost. Now, picture having a clear map with a destination marked, along with specific stops along the way. This makes your journey smoother more enjoyable, and ensures you reach your destination. Setting SMART goals works similarly in managing OCD; it provides a clear path and helps you stay on track. SMART goals are Specific, Measurable, Achievable, Relevant, and Time-bound. These five components make your goals clear and actionable, giving you a sense of direction and purpose.

5.1 UNDERSTANDING SMART GOALS: WHY THEY MATTER

Let's break down what each part of a SMART goal means. First, Specific. A specific goal is clearly defined, leaving no room for ambiguity. Instead of saying, "I want to be healthier," you might say, "I want to work out for 30 minutes three times a week." This clarity helps you know exactly what you need to do. Next, Measurable. This means your goal has criteria for tracking progress. If your goal is to reduce hand-washing, you might measure it by counting how many times you wash your hands each day. Having a measurable goal lets you see how far you've come and what still needs improvement.

Achievable goals are realistic and attainable. Setting a goal to eliminate all OCD symptoms in a week isn't achievable and can lead to frustration. Instead, aim for something within reach, like reducing the time spent on compulsions by 10% over a month. Relevant goals matter to you and align with your values and long-term objectives. If managing OCD is crucial for your mental health, your goals should support this. Finally, Time-bound means setting a deadline for your goal. This creates a sense of urgency and helps you stay focused. For example, you might set a goal to practice ERP exercises for 30 minutes a day, five days a week, for the next month.

Why are SMART goals so effective for personal development? They keep you focused on positive change. By setting clear, actionable steps, you can avoid feeling overwhelmed and stay motivated. SMART goals also provide a sense of control and accomplishment. Each small victory, whether it's reducing a compulsion or sticking to a new routine, builds your confidence and reinforces your progress. This structure helps you see the bigger picture, making it easier to stay committed to your goals.

Let's look at how each component of SMART goals can be applied in managing OCD. Specific goals are clearly defined, leaving no room for misunderstanding. For example, instead of setting a vague goal like "I want to reduce my OCD symptoms," you might say, "I want to practice ERP exercises for 30 minutes a day, five days a week." This specificity makes it clear what you need to do and helps you stay focused. Measurable goals have criteria for tracking progress. If your goal is to reduce checking behaviors, you might measure it by counting how many times you check locks or appliances each day. This allows you to see your progress and make adjustments as needed.

Achievable goals are realistic and within reach. Setting a goal to completely eliminate OCD symptoms in a short time frame isn't realistic and can lead to disappointment. Instead, aim for something attainable, like reducing the time spent on compulsions by 10% over the next month. This makes the goal more manageable and increases the likelihood of success. Relevant goals matter to you and support your long-term objectives. If managing OCD is a priority for your mental health, your goals should align with this. Finally, Time-bound goals have a deadline, creating a sense of urgency and helping you stay on track. For example, you might set a goal to reduce checking behaviors to twice a day within two months.

Setting goals is especially important in managing OCD because it provides direction and motivation. When you have clear goals, you can focus on positive change and avoid feeling overwhelmed by the challenges of OCD. Goals give you something to work towards, making it easier to stay motivated and committed to your progress. They also provide a sense of control and accomplishment, which is crucial for building confidence and resilience. Each small victory, whether it's reducing a compulsion or sticking to a new routine, reinforces your progress and boosts your confidence.

Here are some examples of SMART goals specific to managing OCD. If you're working on reducing hand-washing, a goal might be, "I want to reduce the time spent washing my hands to five minutes per session, three times a day, within the next month." This goal is specific, measurable, achievable, relevant, and time-bound. Another example is for checking behaviors. You might set a goal to "reduce checking behaviors to twice a day within two months." This provides a clear, actionable plan and a deadline to work towards. Practicing ERP exercises is another great area for setting SMART goals. You could aim to "practice ERP exercises for 30 minutes a day, five days a week, for the next month." This structure helps you stay focused and committed, making it easier to see your progress and stay motivated.

By setting SMART goals, you can create a clear path for managing your OCD. These goals provide direction, motivation, and a sense of accomplishment, helping you stay focused on positive change. Remember, the key is to make your goals specific, measurable, achievable, relevant, and time-bound. This framework helps you stay on track and makes it easier to see your progress, building your confidence and resilience along the way.

Reflection Section: Create Your Own SMART Goals

Take a moment to think about areas in your life impacted by OCD. What specific goals can you set to manage these challenges? Use the SMART framework to define your goals clearly. Write down at least two SMART goals you want to achieve in the next month. For example:

- "Practice mindfulness meditation for 10 minutes every morning for the next 30 days."
- "Reduce checking behaviors to twice a day within two months."

Reflect on how achieving these goals will positively impact your life. Keep these goals somewhere visible as a daily reminder of what you're working towards.

5.2 SETTING PERSONAL GOALS: TAILORING TO YOUR NEEDS

When it comes to setting personal goals, it's important to reflect on your individual needs and aspirations. Start by thinking about the areas of your life most impacted by OCD. Maybe it's affecting your schoolwork, social life, or even how you feel about yourself. To get a clearer picture, ask yourself some reflective questions: "What do I want to improve?" "Where do I feel most challenged?" "What would make my daily life more manageable?" These questions can help you pinpoint specific areas to focus on and give you a better understanding of where to start.

Once you've identified the areas you want to work on, it's time to set tailored goals. Begin by assessing your current challenges and strengths. Take a moment to consider what you're good at and where you struggle. For instance, you might be great at sticking to a study schedule but find it hard to resist the urge to check things repeatedly. Knowing your strengths can help you leverage them to tackle your challenges. Prioritize the areas that need the most attention. If checking behaviors interfere with your daily routine, you might prioritize setting goals to reduce these behaviors first.

Creating personalized SMART goals follows a few clear steps. Start by listing specific areas to address. Write down potential goals and refine them using the SMART criteria. For example, if social interactions are challenging, a goal might be, "Attend one social event without performing compulsions by the end of the month." This goal is specific to social interactions, measurable by the number of events attended, achievable within a month, relevant to improving social life, and time-bound with a clear deadline.

To make this process more manageable, use goal-setting worksheets. These tools can help you organize your thoughts and create a structured plan. Begin by listing the specific areas you want to address, such as social interactions, academic performance, or daily routines. For each area, write down potential goals. Then, refine these goals using the SMART criteria. This exercise helps you create clear, actionable goals that are tailored to your needs.

Flexibility is key when setting personal goals. Life is unpredictable, and circumstances can change, so it's important to review and adjust your goals regularly. If a goal proves too challenging or too easy, don't hesitate to modify it. For example, if your goal was to reduce hand-washing to five times a day but you find it overwhelming, adjust it to a more manageable number. The aim is to make progress, not to set yourself up for failure. Regularly reviewing your goals helps you stay on track and make necessary adjustments.

Staying motivated despite setbacks is crucial. Everyone faces obstacles, and it's normal to encounter challenges along the way. When you hit a bump in the road, remind yourself why you set the goal in the first place. Reflect on the progress you've made and how achieving the goal will improve your life. Keep a journal to document your journey, noting down both your successes and the challenges you face. This can provide a sense of accomplishment and help you stay motivated.

To make this more practical, here are some exercises for goal-setting. Start with a brainstorming session. Sit down with a notebook and list all the areas impacted by OCD that you want to improve. Once you have your list, prioritize the areas that need the most attention. Next, create specific goals for each area using the

SMART criteria. Write down these goals in a goal-setting work-sheet, refining them until they are clear and actionable.

For example, let's say you want to improve your academic perfor-mance. Your initial goal might be, "Do better in school." To make it a SMART goal, refine it to "Complete all homework assignments by 8 PM each night for the next two weeks." This goal is specific (homework assignments), measurable (completion by 8 PM), achievable (within two weeks), relevant (improving academic performance), and time-bound (two weeks). Another example could be related to social interactions. If you want to reduce anxiety in social settings, your goal might be, "Attend one social event for at least 30 minutes without performing any compulsions by the end of the month."

By following these steps and using the exercises provided, you can set personal goals that are tailored to your unique needs and aspira-tions. Remember, the key is to create goals that are specific, measurable, achievable, relevant, and time-bound. This framework helps you stay focused, motivated, and on track to achieve your objectives. Keep reviewing and adjusting your goals as needed, and always celebrate your progress along the way.

Interactive Exercise: Personal Goal-Setting Worksheet

Take a moment to create your own personal goals using the SMART criteria. Use the following worksheet to guide you:

1. List specific areas to address (e.g., social interactions, academic performance, daily routines).
2. Write down potential goals for each area.
3. Refine each goal using the SMART criteria.

Example:

Area: Social Interactions

- Initial Goal: "Attend more social events."
- Refined SMART Goal: "Attend one social event for at least 30 minutes without performing any compulsions by the end of the month."

Area: Academic Performance

- Initial Goal: "Do better in school."
- Refined SMART Goal: "Complete all homework assignments by 8 PM each night for the next two weeks."

Reflect on how achieving these goals will impact your life positively and keep your worksheet somewhere visible as a daily reminder of what you're working towards.

5.3 TRACKING PROGRESS: TOOLS AND TECHNIQUES

Keeping track of your progress is like having a personal cheerleader. It not only boosts your motivation but also provides valuable insights into how far you've come and what adjustments you might need to make. When you see tangible improvements, it reinforces the idea that your efforts are paying off. This can be incredibly encouraging, especially when managing something as challenging as OCD. Monitoring your progress helps keep your goals and efforts aligned, ensuring you stay on track and continue moving forward.

There are various tools you can use to track your progress. One of the most straightforward methods is keeping a journal or diary. This allows you to note down your daily achievements, challenges, and observations. For example, you could maintain a daily log of completed ERP exercises. Each entry could include the specific exercise you did, how long you practiced, and any feelings or thoughts you had during the session. This not only helps you track your progress but also provides a space for reflection, which can be therapeutic.

In today's digital age, there are also numerous apps and tools designed to help you track habits and goals. Apps like Habitica and Trello can be incredibly useful. Habitica turns goal tracking into a game where you earn rewards for completing tasks, making the process fun and engaging. Trello, on the other hand, offers customizable boards where you can organize your goals, tasks, and progress. You can create different lists for each goal and move tasks from "To Do" to "Done," providing a clear visual representation of your progress.

Effective progress tracking involves setting regular check-ins and reviews. This helps you stay accountable and make any necessary adjustments to your goals. For instance, you might have a weekly review session where you assess your progress and adjust your goals if needed. During these sessions, take a look at what you've accomplished, identify any obstacles you faced, and think about how you can overcome them. This practice keeps you focused and ensures that your goals remain realistic and achievable.

Visual aids like charts and graphs can also enhance your progress tracking. Creating a progress chart for reducing compulsive behaviors can provide a clear, visual representation of your achievements. For example, you could create a chart that tracks the number of times you engage in a specific compulsion each day. As you see the numbers decrease over time, it serves as a powerful reminder of your progress and motivates you to keep going.

To make this even more practical, here are some ready-to-use templates to help you start tracking your progress. A printable goal-tracking sheet can be a great tool. This sheet could include sections for each goal, the specific actions you need to take, and a space for daily or weekly check-ins. For example, if one of your goals is to practice daily mindfulness, the sheet could have a column for each day of the week where you can tick off whether you completed your practice. Another useful template could be a chart for measuring the reduction in compulsive behaviors over time. This chart could track the frequency of a specific compulsion, providing a clear visual of your progress.

Imagine using a goal-tracking app like Strides. You can set up different trackers for each of your goals, such as reducing hand-washing or practicing ERP exercises. The app provides reminders, progress reports, and even charts to visualize your achievements. Seeing your progress in such a tangible way can be incredibly motivating and helps you stay committed to your goals.

By tracking your progress, you gain a clearer understanding of what's working and what's not. This allows you to make informed adjustments and stay on the path to achieving your goals. Remember, the key is to find a tracking method that works for you, whether it's a journal, an app, or visual aids like charts and graphs. Keep it simple, consistent, and reflective of your unique journey.

5.4 CELEBRATING SMALL WINS: BUILDING CONFIDENCE AND MOTIVATION

Recognizing and celebrating progress, no matter how small, can have a significant impact on your motivation and overall mental well-being. When you take the time to acknowledge your achievements, you boost your morale and reinforce positive behavior. The psychological benefits of celebrating small wins are well-documented. Each small victory releases dopamine, a feel-good neurotransmitter that enhances your mood and encourages you to keep going. This can be especially important when managing OCD, where progress can sometimes feel slow and challenging.

Building confidence through small wins also helps you see that change is possible. When you celebrate even the tiniest steps forward, you build a sense of accomplishment that motivates you to tackle bigger challenges. For instance, if you manage to reduce the time spent on a compulsion by just a few minutes, celebrating this achievement reinforces the positive behavior and boosts your confidence. It's like stacking up small bricks to build a strong foundation for larger successes.

Rewarding yourself for reaching milestones is a great way to stay motivated. Simple rewards can make a big difference. For example, treat yourself to your favorite snack or enjoy some extra screen time when you achieve a goal. These rewards act as positive reinforcement, making the process of managing OCD more enjoyable. You might reward yourself with a movie night after successfully completing a week of ERP practice. This not only gives you something to look forward to but also reinforces the habit of sticking to your goals.

Practicing self-compassion is equally important. Managing OCD is tough, and it's easy to be hard on yourself when things don't go as planned. However, being kind to yourself and acknowledging your efforts can make a huge difference. Techniques for practicing self-compassion include positive self-talk and self-care activities. For instance, when you face a setback, instead of beating yourself up, remind yourself that it's okay to struggle and that you're doing your best. You might write a letter of encouragement to yourself, acknowledging your efforts and reminding yourself of your progress.

Let's look at some real-life stories to illustrate the impact of recognizing progress. Meet Emma, who struggled with checking rituals. After her first week without performing these rituals, Emma decided to celebrate by treating herself to a day at the park with her favorite book. This small celebration boosted her confidence and motivated her to keep pushing forward. Then there's Jake, who dealt with intrusive thoughts about harm. After successfully reducing these thoughts, Jake rewarded himself with a day trip to his favorite hiking trail. The reward not only celebrated his progress but also provided a relaxing and enjoyable experience that reinforced his efforts.

Lily's experience is another great example. Lily had a goal to reduce her compulsive behaviors around symmetry and order. After achieving her goal, she treated herself to a new book she'd been wanting to read. This simple reward acknowledged her hard work and gave her something enjoyable to focus on, further motivating her to maintain her progress. These stories show that celebrating small wins can make a significant difference in managing OCD.

As we wrap up this chapter, remember that celebrating small wins is not just about the rewards but also about building confidence and reinforcing positive behavior. Each small victory adds up, creating a strong foundation for bigger successes. Keep acknowledging your progress, be kind to yourself, and stay motivated. The next chapter will explore how exercise and nutrition can further support your mental health and well-being.

EXERCISE AND NUTRITION FOR MENTAL HEALTH

I magine you're having one of those days where everything feels overwhelming. Your mind is racing with intrusive thoughts, and the urge to perform compulsions feels stronger than ever. Now, picture yourself lacing up a pair of running shoes and heading outside for a jog. As you start running, the rhythm of your feet hitting the pavement begins to clear your mind. You feel the tension in your body easing, and for a moment, the noise in your head quiets down. This isn't just a coincidence; it's the power of exercise working its magic on your mental health.

THE CONNECTION BETWEEN EXERCISE AND MENTAL HEALTH

Regular exercise does wonders for your mental well-being. When you engage in physical activity, your body releases endorphins, often referred to as "feel-good" hormones. These endorphins interact with receptors in your brain, reducing your perception of pain and triggering positive feelings. Think of them as natural mood lifters that can help combat anxiety and improve your overall mood. Exercise also helps lower levels of cortisol, a stress hormone that can wreak havoc on your mind and body when present in high amounts. By reducing cortisol, exercise helps alleviate stress, making it easier to handle daily challenges.

Another significant benefit of regular exercise is improved sleep quality. Physical activity tires out your body, making it easier to fall asleep and stay asleep throughout the night. Better sleep, in turn, enhances your mood, reduces stress, and improves cognitive function. It's a positive cycle where each element reinforces the other, leading to better mental health overall.

But how does exercise specifically impact OCD symptoms? For starters, it serves as a powerful distraction from intrusive thoughts. When you're focused on a physical activity, whether it's running, swimming, or playing a sport, your mind has less room to dwell on obsessions. This break from incessant thoughts can provide much-needed relief. Exercise also helps reduce the frequency and intensity of compulsions. For example, a teen who uses running to manage their checking behaviors might find that the urge to check decreases after a good run. Physical activity channels your energy into something positive, reducing the hold OCD has on you.

Scientific evidence backs up the mental health benefits of exercise. A systematic review and meta-analysis published in 2022 found that exercise significantly reduces OCD symptoms. The analysis included randomized controlled trials and pre-post trials, showing a large reduction in OCD symptoms following exercise interventions. The study also highlighted significant decreases in anxiety and depression, further emphasizing the positive impact of physical activity on mental health. These findings support the idea that exercise is a valuable tool in managing OCD and improving overall well-being.

Real-life stories provide compelling evidence of exercise's benefits. Take Emma, for example. Emma struggled with anxiety and intrusive thoughts, making it hard for her to focus on schoolwork or enjoy social activities. She decided to try yoga as a way to calm her mind. Through regular practice, Emma found that yoga helped her manage her anxiety and reduce the intensity of her intrusive thoughts. The combination of physical movement and mindfulness provided a sense of peace and control that she hadn't experienced before.

Then there's Jake, who found relief through team sports. Jake's OCD manifested in compulsive counting and tapping behaviors. He joined his school's basketball team, hoping that the physical activity would help. To his surprise, playing basketball did more than just keep him fit. The focus required during games and practices provided a distraction from his compulsions. Additionally, the camaraderie and support from his teammates boosted his confidence and reduced his overall anxiety.

Testimonials from other teens further illustrate the impact of exercise on managing OCD. One teen shared how running helped them cope with their checking behaviors. They described how the rhythmic nature of running provided a mental escape from their compulsions. Another teen found that weightlifting helped them channel their energy into something productive, reducing the time spent on rituals. These stories highlight the diverse ways exercise can be tailored to fit individual needs and preferences, offering a versatile tool for managing OCD.

Incorporating exercise into your routine can be a game-changer for your mental health. Whether it's yoga, team sports, running, or any other form of physical activity, the benefits are clear. From reducing anxiety and stress to improving sleep and mood, exercise offers a holistic approach to enhancing your well-being. So, the next time you feel overwhelmed by intrusive thoughts or compulsions, consider lacing up your running shoes or hitting the yoga mat. Your mind and body will thank you.

CREATING AN EXERCISE ROUTINE: TIPS AND TRICKS

Starting an exercise routine can feel like a big task, but breaking it down into manageable steps makes it easier. First, think about your current fitness level and interests. Are you someone who loves being outdoors, or do you prefer indoor activities? Do you have any physical limitations or injuries? Understanding where you're starting from helps you set realistic goals. For example, if you're new to exercise, you might begin with something simple like 20-minute walks. As you get more comfortable, you can gradually increase the intensity and duration. The key is to start small and build up over time.

Variety is the spice of life, and it's especially true for exercise. Different types of physical activities can keep things interesting and ensure you're working various muscle groups. Aerobic exercises like running, swimming, and cycling are great for getting your heart rate up and improving cardiovascular health. If you enjoy the water, swimming can be both relaxing and invigorating. If you prefer being on land, cycling offers a fantastic way to explore your surroundings while getting fit. Strength training is another excellent option. This can include bodyweight exercises like push-ups and squats or lifting weights. Building muscle not only makes you stronger but also boosts your metabolism. Then there are flexibility and balance exercises like yoga and Pilates. These activities improve your range of motion and help prevent injuries, making them a perfect complement to more intense workouts.

Staying motivated can be one of the biggest challenges when it comes to maintaining an exercise routine. Finding a workout buddy can make a huge difference. Having someone to exercise with provides accountability and makes the experience more enjoyable. You can encourage each other, share progress, and even engage in a bit of friendly competition. Another way to keep things fun is by creating an exercise playlist. Choose songs that pump you up and make you want to move. Music has a powerful effect on mood and can make your workouts feel more like a dance party than a chore. Setting up a reward system can also be motivating. For example, treat yourself to a smoothie or a favorite snack after completing a week of consistent workouts. Rewards give you something to look forward to and celebrate your dedication.

Balancing exercise with rest is crucial for avoiding burnout and injury. Your body needs time to recover and repair itself after physical activity. Overtraining can lead to persistent fatigue, irritability, and even injuries, which can set you back in your fitness journey. Incorporating rest days into your routine is vital. Use these days to engage in gentle activities like stretching or taking a leisurely walk. This keeps you active without putting too much strain on your body. Listening to your body is essential. If you're feeling unusually tired or sore, it might be a sign that you need more rest. Pushing through pain can do more harm than good, so it's important to give your body the time it needs to heal.

Creating a personalized exercise routine that fits your interests and lifestyle makes it more likely that you'll stick with it. Start by assessing your current fitness level and interests, and then set realistic goals. Incorporate a variety of exercises to keep things interesting and ensure you're working different muscle groups. Stay motivated by finding a workout buddy, creating a fun playlist, and setting up a reward system. Remember to balance exercise with rest, giving your body the recovery time it needs to stay strong and healthy. With these tips and tricks, you're well on your way to making exercise a regular and enjoyable part of your life.

NUTRITION AND OCD: FOODS THAT HELP AND HURT

Think about the last time you felt really sluggish or moody. Chances are, what you ate (or didn't eat) played a big role in that. Your diet has a huge impact on your brain function and mood. Nutrients like omega-3 fatty acids and antioxidants are crucial for brain health. Omega-3s, found in foods like salmon and flaxseeds, help build cell membranes in the brain and reduce inflammation, which can improve mood and cognitive function. Antioxidants, found in berries and leafy greens, protect your brain from oxidative stress, which can harm brain cells and affect your mental health. Keeping your blood sugar levels stable is another important factor. When you eat foods that cause rapid spikes and crashes in blood sugar, like sugary snacks, you're more likely to experience mood swings and energy dips. A balanced diet with complex carbohydrates, protein, and healthy fats can help stabilize your blood sugar and keep your mood steady.

Specific foods can make a real difference in managing OCD symptoms. For example, foods rich in omega-3 fatty acids, like salmon and flaxseeds, support brain health and reduce inflammation, which can help improve your mood and cognitive function. Antioxidant-rich fruits and vegetables, such as berries and leafy greens, protect your brain from oxidative stress and promote overall mental health. Whole grains and complex carbohydrates, like quinoa and brown rice, provide steady energy and help keep your blood sugar levels stable, reducing the likelihood of mood swings and anxiety. Including these foods in your diet can help create a more supportive environment for managing OCD symptoms.

On the flip side, some foods can make OCD symptoms worse. High-sugar and high-fat foods are the culprits here. Consuming a lot of sugary snacks and drinks can cause spikes and crashes in your blood sugar levels, leading to mood swings and increased anxiety. Caffeine is another common trigger. While a cup of coffee or soda might give you a temporary boost, it can also increase anxiety and make it harder to manage intrusive thoughts. Processed foods and artificial additives, often found in fast food and packaged snacks, can also negatively impact your mental health. These foods are usually low in nutrients and high in unhealthy fats, sugars, and chemicals that can exacerbate symptoms of anxiety and OCD. Being mindful of what you eat and making healthier choices can help you feel better both physically and mentally.

Making healthier food choices doesn't have to be complicated. Start by planning balanced meals and snacks that include a mix of protein, healthy fats, and complex carbohydrates. This can help keep your energy levels steady and your mood stable. Reading food labels is another useful habit. Look for ingredients you recognize and avoid those with long lists of artificial additives and sugars. For example, instead of grabbing a sugary snack like candy or soda, opt for healthier alternatives like nuts, fruit, or yogurt. These options provide essential nutrients and energy without the negative effects of sugar crashes. Small changes in your diet can have a big impact on your mental health.

Emma noticed significant improvements in her OCD symptoms after making dietary changes. She started incorporating more omega-3-rich foods like salmon and walnuts into her meals. She also added a variety of antioxidant-rich fruits and vegetables to her diet. Within a few weeks, Emma felt more balanced and noticed a reduction in her intrusive thoughts. Jake, on the other hand, decided to cut down on sugary snacks and drinks. He swapped his daily soda for water and replaced candy with fresh fruit. Jake found that his mood became more stable, and he experienced fewer compulsions. These small changes in their diets helped Emma and Jake manage their OCD symptoms more effectively.

Planning balanced meals and snacks can feel like a big task, but it's worth the effort. Start by making a weekly meal plan that includes a variety of nutrient-dense foods. This helps you avoid last-minute unhealthy choices and ensures you're getting the nutrients your brain needs. When grocery shopping, make a list based on your meal plan to stay focused and avoid impulse buys. Buying in bulk for staples like grains, legumes, and nuts can also save money and ensure you have healthy options on hand. Seasonal fruits and vegetables are often more affordable and fresher, making them a great choice for your meals.

Remember to pay attention to food labels and choose options with recognizable ingredients. Avoid products with long lists of artificial additives and sugars. Swapping sugary snacks for healthier alternatives like nuts, fruit, or yogurt can help keep your energy levels steady and support your mental health. Small changes in your diet can make a big difference in how you feel and manage your OCD symptoms.

MEAL PLANNING FOR MENTAL CLARITY: PRACTICAL ADVICE

Imagine you wake up late, rush out the door, and grab a donut for breakfast. By mid-morning, you're already feeling sluggish and distracted. Now, think about starting your day with a nutritious meal planned out in advance. You have more energy, focus better, and feel more balanced. This is the power of meal planning. Creating a weekly meal plan is a game-changer for your mental health. It ensures you get balanced meals with the right mix of protein, carbs, and fats, providing the steady energy and nutrients your brain needs to function optimally. Planning meals ahead also helps you avoid last-minute, unhealthy choices that can leave you feeling drained and irritable.

To get started with meal planning, grab a template or create your own. Begin by listing out meals for each day of the week. Think about incorporating a variety of foods to keep things interesting and ensure you're getting a wide range of nutrients. Aim for balanced meals that include a source of protein, healthy fats, and complex carbohydrates. For example, plan a breakfast of scrambled eggs (protein) with avocado (healthy fats) and whole-grain toast (complex carbs). For lunch, consider a quinoa salad with mixed veggies and grilled chicken. Dinner might be baked salmon with a side of roasted vegetables and brown rice. By planning ahead, you set yourself up for success, making it easier to stick to healthy eating habits.

Quick and easy recipes are your best friend when it comes to staying on track with your meal plan. For breakfast, try overnight oats. Mix rolled oats with your choice of milk, a spoonful of chia seeds, and a handful of berries. Let it sit in the fridge overnight, and in the morning, you have a delicious and nutritious meal ready to go. Another great option is smoothie bowls. Blend your favorite fruits with some yogurt and top it with granola and nuts. For lunch, quinoa salad is both satisfying and easy to prepare. Cook quinoa according to the package instructions, then toss it with chopped veggies, a protein source like turkey or tofu, and a simple dressing. Turkey wraps are another quick lunch idea. Spread some hummus on a whole-grain wrap, add sliced turkey, fresh veggies, and roll it up. For dinner, try baked salmon with veggies. Place a salmon filet on a baking sheet, drizzle with olive oil, and season with salt, pepper, and your favorite herbs. Add some chopped veggies to the sheet and bake at 400°F for about 20 minutes. Stir-fry is another versatile option. Sauté your choice of veggies and protein in a bit of olive oil, add a splash of soy sauce, and serve over brown rice or noodles.

Eating healthy doesn't have to break the bank. With a few smart strategies, you can buy nutritious foods without overspending. Start by making a shopping list based on your meal plan. This helps you stay focused and avoid impulse buys. Buying in bulk is another great way to save money. Stock up on staples like grains, legumes, and nuts, which have a long shelf life and can be used in various recipes. Choosing seasonal fruits and vegetables is also cost-effective. They're often cheaper and fresher than out-of-season produce. For example, in the summer, berries and tomatoes are abundant and affordable, while in the winter, root vegetables like carrots and sweet potatoes are great options. Shopping at local farmers' markets can also provide fresh produce at lower prices.

Mindful eating practices can transform your relationship with food, making meals more enjoyable and satisfying. Start by paying attention to your hunger and fullness cues. Eat when you're hungry and stop when you're full. This helps you avoid overeating and ensures you get the right amount of nutrients. Avoid distractions while eating, like watching TV or scrolling through your phone. Instead, focus on the taste, texture, and aroma of your food. This not only enhances your enjoyment but also helps your body recognize when it's full. Practicing gratitude before meals is another powerful tool. Take a moment to appreciate the food on your plate and the effort that went into preparing it. This simple act can make you more mindful of your eating habits and foster a positive relationship with food.

With these meal planning tips, you can create nutritious, balanced meals that support your mental clarity and overall well-being. From planning ahead to mindful eating practices, these strategies help you make healthier choices, improve your mood, and manage OCD symptoms more effectively. So, grab a meal planning template, jot down your favorite recipes, and get ready to take control of your nutrition and mental health.

REAL-LIFE CASE STUDIES AND TESTIMONIALS

✥

I magine sitting in a classroom, trying to focus on your lesson, but all you can think about is whether your hands are clean enough. This was Emma's reality every single day. Emma is a bright, ambitious teenager who dreams of becoming a doctor. However, her severe anxiety about contamination made school a nightmare. She worried incessantly about germs, convinced that even the slightest touch could make her dangerously ill. This fear led her to wash her hands countless times a day, often until her skin was raw and bleeding. Emma's life was consumed by her need to feel clean, and this compulsion started to take a toll on her academic performance and social interactions.

Emma's fear of contamination was so intense that it affected every aspect of her school life. She couldn't touch her desk or books without feeling the urgent need to wash her hands. This made it nearly impossible for her to concentrate on her studies. Her grades began to slip, and she found herself falling behind in subjects she once excelled in. Socially, things weren't much better. Emma avoided touching doorknobs, shaking hands, or participating in group activities. Her friends didn't understand why she acted this way, which made her feel isolated and misunderstood. The anxiety was so overwhelming that she often skipped school to avoid dealing with her fears.

When Emma finally sought help, she was introduced to Cognitive Behavioral Therapy (CBT) and Exposure and Response Prevention (ERP). These therapies became game-changers for her. CBT helped her understand the connection between her thoughts, feelings, and behaviors. She learned to identify the irrational thoughts that fueled her anxiety and began to challenge them. ERP, on the other hand, involved gradually exposing herself to the things she feared while resisting the urge to wash her hands. At first, this was incredibly difficult. Emma started small—she would touch her desk without immediately washing her hands. This exposure made her anxious, but over time, she noticed that the anxiety began to decrease. She created a fear hierarchy, ranking her triggers from least to most anxiety-provoking, and slowly worked her way through the list.

Emma's progress wasn't something she achieved alone. Her family played a crucial role in her recovery. Her parents attended therapy sessions with her and learned how to support her without enabling her compulsions. They encouraged her to stick to her ERP exercises and celebrated her small victories. Emma's school counselor also provided invaluable support. The counselor helped create a plan that allowed Emma to ease back into school activities at her own pace. Friends who understood her struggles offered moral support, making her feel less alone.

With this robust support system, Emma's life began to change. Her academic performance improved as she spent less time consumed by her compulsions and more time focusing on her studies. She felt more confident participating in class and engaging in group projects. Emma also started to enjoy school activities again. She joined the school debate team, something she had always wanted to do but had avoided because of her anxiety. This newfound involvement boosted her self-esteem and gave her a sense of normalcy that she had longed for.

Emma's journey wasn't easy, but the progress she made was remarkable. By using CBT and ERP, she learned to manage her OCD symptoms effectively. Her fear of contamination no longer controlled her life, and she regained the confidence to pursue her dreams. Emma's story is a testament to the power of effective therapy, a strong support system, and sheer determination. It shows that while OCD can be incredibly challenging, it is manageable with the right tools and support.

JAKE'S JOURNEY: MANAGING SOCIAL FEARS

Jake is a 15-year-old who has always found social situations incredibly daunting. His intense fear of saying or doing something embarrassing manifested as OCD, making his everyday interactions a minefield of anxiety. Jake's OCD primarily revolved around social fears. He would spend hours rehearsing conversations in his head, trying to predict every possible outcome to avoid any embarrassing mistakes. This compulsion made him avoid eye contact, which he feared would make others think he was weird or awkward. These behaviors severely impacted his ability to make and maintain friendships. Jake often felt isolated, convinced that any social misstep would lead to ridicule or rejection.

To tackle his social anxiety, Jake was introduced to Dialectical Behavior Therapy (DBT), a therapeutic approach that focuses on emotion regulation, mindfulness, and distress tolerance. DBT was a game-changer for Jake, especially with its emphasis on balancing acceptance and change. One of the first skills Jake learned was mindfulness. By practicing mindfulness, he could stay present in the moment and observe his thoughts without getting overwhelmed. This helped him reduce the power of his intrusive thoughts, making social situations less intimidating. Another crucial component of DBT for Jake was distress tolerance. He learned the "TIPP" skills—Temperature, Intense Exercise, Paced Breathing, and Progressive Relaxation. Before social events, Jake would splash cold water on his face to change his body temperature and calm his nervous system. If the anxiety felt too intense, he'd do a quick set of jumping jacks to release some of that pent-up energy. Practicing paced breathing and progressive relaxation helped him manage his anxiety more effectively, making it easier for him to face social situations without feeling overwhelmed.

Jake's journey was made easier with the support of his peers. Finding a supportive friend group through a school club was a turning point for him. These friends understood his struggles and never made him feel judged. They even helped Jake role-play social scenarios, giving him a safe space to practice conversations and eye contact. This practice was invaluable, as it allowed Jake to build his confidence in a controlled environment. Participating in group therapy sessions with other teens dealing with similar issues also provided a sense of community and understanding. Knowing he wasn't alone in his struggles made a significant difference in Jake's outlook.

As Jake continued to practice DBT skills and receive support from his peers, his confidence in social interactions grew. He no longer felt the need to rehearse every conversation or avoid eye contact. Instead, he could engage more naturally and enjoy the company of others. This newfound confidence led to the formation of meaningful friendships. Jake found himself surrounded by people who appreciated him for who he was, quirks and all. One of Jake's most significant achievements was leading a project in his school's community service club. This was something he never thought he could do because of his social fears. But with the skills he learned in DBT and the support of his friends, Jake took on the challenge and excelled. Leading the project not only boosted his confidence but also gave him a sense of accomplishment and purpose.

Jake's journey with OCD and social anxiety highlights the importance of effective therapy and a strong support system. By learning and practicing DBT skills, he managed to reduce his anxiety and improve his social interactions. The support from his peers provided the encouragement and understanding he needed to push through his fears. Today, Jake is more confident, socially engaged, and ready to take on new challenges. His story is a testament to the power of resilience, the right therapeutic approaches, and the importance of having a supportive network.

LILY'S TRIUMPH: BALANCING OCD AND SPORTS

Lily loved sports. She was the kind of person who thrived on the rush of adrenaline, the camaraderie of her teammates, and the thrill of competition. But her OCD had other plans. Lily's perfectionism and fear of making mistakes turned what should have been a joyful experience into a source of stress and anxiety. She found herself compulsively checking her sports equipment multiple times before every game and practice. Her anxiety about performance was so overwhelming that she feared judgment from her teammates if she made even the smallest error. This constant worry drained her enjoyment of the game and impacted her overall performance.

Instead of focusing on her skills and the fun of playing, she was trapped in a cycle of checking, doubting, and self-criticism.

To manage her OCD while continuing to play sports, Lily turned to Acceptance and Commitment Therapy (ACT). ACT focuses on values-based actions and helps individuals accept their intrusive thoughts rather than fighting them. This approach was particularly helpful for Lily because it allowed her to focus on what truly mattered to her—her love for sports and her desire to be a good teammate. One of the techniques she learned in ACT was cognitive defusion, which involves seeing thoughts as just thoughts, not truths that need to be acted upon. For instance, before games, Lily practiced the "Leaves on a stream" exercise. She would visualize her intrusive thoughts as leaves floating down a stream, acknowledging them without letting them dictate her actions. This exercise helped her reduce the power of her thoughts, allowing her to concentrate on playing rather than worrying.

Lily's journey wasn't something she tackled alone. Her coaches and teammates played a crucial role in her recovery. Open communication with her coach was a game-changer. She explained her OCD and how it affected her performance. Her coach responded with understanding and support, encouraging her to focus on her strengths and reminding her that mistakes were a part of learning. This open dialogue made Lily feel less isolated and more confident in her ability to manage her OCD on the field. Her teammates were equally supportive. They practiced mindfulness exercises together, creating a team culture that valued mental well-being. Knowing that her teammates had her back made it easier for Lily to face her fears and reduce her compulsions.

With the support of her sports community and the strategies she learned in ACT, Lily's performance began to improve. She found herself less preoccupied with checking her equipment and more focused on the game. Her anxiety during games decreased, and she started to play with the confidence and joy she once had. Her dedication and perseverance didn't go unnoticed. Lily won a sportsmanship award for her efforts, recognizing not just her athletic skills but also her resilience in managing her OCD. This award was a testament to her hard work and the progress she had made. It boosted her self-esteem and reinforced her commitment to both her sport and her mental health.

Lily's renewed passion for sports was evident in her increased participation in team activities. She no longer avoided team events for fear of making mistakes or being judged. Instead, she embraced every opportunity to bond with her teammates and improve her skills. Her love for the game was rekindled, and she played with a sense of freedom she hadn't felt in a long time. Her story highlights the power of effective therapy, open communication, and a supportive community. Through ACT and the unwavering support of her coaches and teammates, Lily learned to manage her OCD and rediscover the joy of playing sports.

ALEX'S EXPERIENCE: BUILDING SUPPORTIVE FRIENDSHIPS

Alex always found it difficult to form and maintain friendships. His fear of contamination kept him from engaging in activities that most teens take for granted. He was constantly worried about germs and avoided physical contact, steering clear of handshakes, hugs, and even casual high-fives. Public places were a nightmare for him—he felt the need to carry hand sanitizer everywhere and would often clean surfaces before touching them. These compulsions affected his social life significantly, making him feel isolated and different from his peers. The impact on his friendships was severe. He couldn't join in on spontaneous plans or hang out in crowded places without feeling anxious. This led to feelings of loneliness and a sense of being misunderstood.

To tackle these challenges, Alex turned to Exposure and Response Prevention (ERP), a type of Cognitive Behavioral Therapy specifically designed for OCD. ERP involves gradually exposing oneself to feared situations while refraining from engaging in compulsive behaviors. Alex started small, setting SMART goals to guide his progress. His first goal was to spend five minutes in a public place without using hand sanitizer. It was tough, but he managed it. Gradually, he increased the time he spent in social settings, each time resisting the urge to perform his usual rituals. For instance, he started attending small gatherings, first for just ten minutes, then extending it to half an hour, and so on. This gradual exposure helped him build tolerance to his anxiety and reduced his compulsions over time.

Alex's improvement wasn't solely due to therapy; his support network played a crucial role. His family was incredibly understanding and encouraging. They attended therapy sessions with him, learning how to support his efforts without enabling his compulsions. They celebrated his small victories, like spending an evening out without needing to sanitize everything. Alex also had friends who respected his boundaries and supported his efforts to manage his OCD. One close friend even practiced ERP exercises with him, making it a team effort. They would go to a café, and his friend would encourage him to touch the table and resist the urge to clean it immediately. This kind of support made a significant difference in his progress.

The combination of therapy and a supportive network led to meaningful changes in Alex's life. He began to form deep and meaningful friendships, built on mutual understanding and respect. His confidence in social settings grew, and he no longer felt the need to avoid physical contact or public places. One of his proudest moments was hosting a small gathering for friends at his home. He had always feared the germs that others might bring into his space, but this time, he focused on the joy of being surrounded by friends. The gathering was a success, and it marked a turning point in his social life. Alex realized that he could enjoy social interactions without being governed by his OCD.

Alex's story is a powerful example of how effective therapy and a strong support system can transform the experience of living with OCD. By gradually exposing himself to his fears and building a network of supportive friends and family, he was able to overcome significant social challenges. His journey highlights the importance of perseverance, the right therapeutic approaches, and the invaluable role that understanding and support play in managing OCD.

CONCLUSION

In this chapter, we've seen how real teens like Emma, Jake, Lily, and Alex have successfully managed their OCD with the help of evidence-based therapies and strong support systems. Their stories show that while OCD can be incredibly challenging, it is possible to lead a fulfilling life with the right tools and support. Up next, we'll explore how family dynamics and support play a crucial role in managing OCD, offering practical advice for both teens and their families.

FAMILY DYNAMICS AND SUPPORT

Picture this: you're sitting at the dinner table, trying to enjoy a meal with your family. But in the back of your mind, you're consumed with worry about whether you washed your hands properly. You excuse yourself to wash them again, and again, your family looks puzzled. They might not understand why you have to do this. This lack of understanding can make managing OCD even harder. That's why educating your family about OCD is so important. When your family understands what you're going through, they can provide better support and reduce the misconceptions and stigma surrounding OCD.

EDUCATING YOUR FAMILY: SHARING WHAT YOU'VE LEARNED

First, let's talk about why family education is crucial. When your family understands OCD, they can offer more effective support. Many people think OCD is just about being neat or organized, but it's much more than that. OCD involves unwanted and intrusive thoughts (obsessions) and repetitive behaviors or mental acts (compulsions) that you feel driven to perform. By educating your family, you can help them recognize the signs and symptoms of OCD, which makes it easier for them to support you. For example, they'll understand that your need to wash your hands repeatedly isn't just a quirk but a way to manage overwhelming anxiety.

Education also helps reduce misconceptions and stigma. Many people still believe that individuals with OCD can simply "snap out of it" or "just stop" their behaviors. These misconceptions can lead to frustration, shame, and guilt for both you and your family. By providing accurate information, you can help dispel these myths and create a more supportive environment. For instance, you can explain that OCD is a chronic mental illness that requires professional treatment, just like any other medical condition. This understanding can foster empathy and patience within your family.

To educate your family effectively, suggest some reputable resources they can explore. Books like *"When a Family Member Has OCD: Mindful Parenting and Support"* by Jon Hershfield and *"Freeing Your Child from Obsessive-Compulsive Disorder"* by Tamar Chansky are excellent starting points. These books offer insights into the challenges of living with OCD and practical advice for family members. Online resources like the International OCD Foundation (iocdf.org) provide a wealth of information, including articles, expert opinions, and forums where families can connect with others facing similar challenges. Additionally, local or online support groups can be invaluable. These groups offer a safe space for family members to share their experiences, ask questions, and learn from others who understand what they're going through.

Encouraging open discussions about OCD can also make a big difference. Start by sharing your personal experiences and challenges with OCD. This might feel daunting, but it can help your family understand what you're going through. Consider setting up a family meeting to discuss OCD and its impact on your life. During this meeting, encourage your family members to ask questions and express their concerns. This open dialogue can foster a sense of understanding and collaboration. For example, you might share that intrusive thoughts about contamination are why you wash your hands so often, and explain how this affects your daily life. By being open and honest, you can help your family see the situation from your perspective.

To make these discussions more effective, include some exercises that can help your family understand OCD better. Role-playing scenarios can be a fun and educational way to demonstrate OCD behaviors. For example, you can act out a situation where you feel the need to check the locks multiple times, while a family member plays the role of someone who doesn't understand why. This exercise can help them see the frustration and anxiety you experience. Another useful activity is practicing ERP techniques together. You can guide your family through an ERP exercise, such as touching a doorknob without washing hands afterward, to show them how challenging but essential these practices are. Watching educational videos or documentaries on OCD as a family can also be enlightening. These visual aids can provide a deeper understanding of the disorder and spark meaningful conversations.

Creating a family plan for handling OCD can be another helpful step. This plan might include specific ways your family can support you, such as reminding you to use coping strategies or celebrating your successes. It could also outline how to handle setbacks and challenges, ensuring everyone is on the same page. For example, the plan might state that if you feel overwhelmed by intrusive thoughts, a family member will sit with you and practice a mindfulness exercise. Having a clear, agreed-upon plan can reduce misunderstandings and provide a sense of stability.

By educating your family about OCD, encouraging open discussions, and involving them in supportive activities, you can create a more understanding and empathetic home environment. This support can make a significant difference in managing your OCD and improving your overall well-being. Remember, your family wants to help, and with the right knowledge and tools, they can be a powerful source of support.

BUILDING A SUPPORTIVE HOME ENVIRONMENT

Imagine walking into a home that feels like a sanctuary, where you can let your guard down and breathe a little easier. This kind of supportive environment can make a huge difference in managing OCD. A positive and understanding atmosphere at home can significantly reduce stress and anxiety triggers, making it easier to cope with obsessive thoughts and compulsive behaviors. When your family creates a calm and organized living space, it can help you feel more in control and less overwhelmed. For instance, having a tidy, clutter-free environment can reduce the chaos that might trigger anxiety. This doesn't mean everything has to be perfect, but a little organization can go a long way in creating a sense of calm.

Open communication and emotional support are also crucial. When you know you can talk to your family about your struggles without fear of judgment, it can be incredibly comforting. This kind of emotional safety net can help you feel less isolated and more understood. Imagine having a family that listens when you need to vent or offers a hug when you're feeling overwhelmed. This kind of support can make facing the challenges of OCD feel a little less daunting.

Creating a supportive home environment involves specific, practical steps. One of the most effective ways is to establish routines and consistency in daily activities. A predictable routine can provide a sense of stability and control, which is particularly helpful when dealing with OCD. For example, having set times for meals, homework, and relaxation can create a structured environment that reduces anxiety. Another practical tip is to set up designated spaces for relaxation and mindfulness practice. A "quiet corner" with comfortable seating, soft lighting, and perhaps some calming elements like plants or a small water fountain can be a perfect spot for meditation or deep breathing exercises. This space can serve as a sanctuary where you can retreat when you need a break from the stressors of daily life.

Family involvement in treatment plans can also make a significant difference. When family members actively participate in your treatment routines, it creates a sense of teamwork and shared responsibility. They can attend therapy sessions or support groups with you, which can provide them with a better understanding of what you're going through and how they can help. Participating in ERP exercises as a family can be particularly powerful. For example, if touching doorknobs triggers your OCD, your family can practice touching doorknobs together and refraining from washing hands afterward. This collective effort can make the process less intimidating and more manageable.

Handling setbacks and challenges is an inevitable part of managing OCD, but having a supportive family can make it easier. Offering encouragement and positive reinforcement during tough times can boost your morale and motivation. It's important for family members to avoid criticism or blame during setbacks. Instead, they should focus on providing constructive support. For example, if you experience an OCD flare-up, a family plan for handling these situations can be incredibly helpful. This plan might include specific steps that family members can take to support you, such as practicing deep breathing exercises together or taking a walk to help clear your mind. Having a predetermined plan can reduce the stress and uncertainty that often accompany setbacks.

Families can also create a supportive environment by setting clear boundaries and expectations. This means finding a balance between being supportive and allowing you to take responsibility for your treatment. For instance, while it's helpful for family members to remind you to practice coping strategies, they should avoid taking over your responsibilities. Encouraging you to take an active role in your treatment fosters independence and builds confidence. At the same time, family members should be prepared to step in with support when needed, ensuring that the balance between support and independence is maintained.

In summary, building a supportive home environment involves creating a calm and organized living space, establishing routines, and encouraging open communication. Family involvement in treatment plans and handling setbacks with encouragement and positive reinforcement can make a significant difference in managing OCD. With the right support, you can create a home environment that feels like a sanctuary, where you can face the challenges of OCD with confidence and resilience.

EFFECTIVE COMMUNICATION: TALKING ABOUT OCD WITHOUT JUDGMENT

Navigating conversations about OCD with your family can feel like walking a tightrope. The key to making these conversations productive is non-judgmental communication. When you talk about your OCD, it's important that your family uses empathetic and supportive language. Instead of saying something like, "Why can't you just stop?" which can come off as dismissive, they should try saying, "I understand this is hard for you." This shows that they are trying to empathize with your experience rather than judge it. Avoiding blame is crucial. Blaming you for your symptoms or behaviors can make you feel even more isolated and misunderstood. Instead, your family should focus on understanding and supporting you.

Active listening is another essential part of effective communication. It's not just about hearing words but really understanding what you're saying. Your family members can start by making eye contact and showing genuine interest in the conversation. This simple act can make you feel seen and heard. Reflecting back what you've said can also show that they understand your perspective. For example, if you're sharing how overwhelmed you feel by a particular thought, they might say, "It sounds like you're feeling really overwhelmed by this thought." This not only shows that they're listening but also validates your feelings.

Validation of emotions is incredibly important. When you're dealing with OCD, your emotions can be all over the place. Having someone acknowledge and validate what you're feeling can be a huge relief. Your family should recognize your struggles and fears. They might say something like, "It's okay to feel anxious about this; it's a normal part of OCD." This kind of reassurance can make you feel less alone in your experience. Offering comfort, like a hug or a kind word, can go a long way in helping you feel supported.

Improving communication skills takes practice, and there are exercises families can do together to get better at it. Role-playing difficult conversations about OCD can be a great way to prepare for real-life discussions. For instance, you can practice how to respond supportively when you disclose an intrusive thought. This can help your family learn the best ways to respond in a supportive manner. Setting aside regular family time for open discussions can also be beneficial. This gives everyone a chance to talk about their feelings and experiences in a safe and supportive environment.

PARENTAL GUIDANCE: HOW PARENTS CAN HELP WITHOUT OVERSTEPPING

Imagine you're climbing a mountain, and your parents are there to support you. They can offer you a hand when you stumble, but they can't climb the mountain for you. This balance between support and independence is crucial when it comes to managing OCD. Parents need to encourage you to take an active role in your treatment. This means supporting your use of coping strategies rather than doing things for you. For example, if you have a ritual of checking the door lock multiple times, instead of checking it for you, your parents can remind you to use a breathing technique to manage your anxiety. This approach helps you build the skills you need to manage OCD independently while still feeling supported.

Providing guidance without being overly controlling is another important aspect. Parents can offer suggestions and advice, but they should avoid dictating every action you take. For instance, they can help you set realistic goals and break down large tasks into manageable steps. If you're feeling overwhelmed by a big project at school, your parents can sit down with you and create a step-by-step plan. This not only makes the task more manageable but also empowers you to take control of your responsibilities. Offering praise and encouragement for your efforts and progress, no matter how small, can boost your confidence and motivation. Hearing "I'm proud of you for working on your ERP exercises today" can make a world of difference.

Respecting boundaries is crucial for maintaining a healthy relationship and fostering independence. Parents should avoid intrusive questioning or demands that might make you feel pressured or judged. For example, giving you space to practice ERP exercises on your own shows that they trust you to handle your treatment. Recognizing when to step back and allow you to handle situations independently is essential. If you're trying to manage your anxiety about a social event, your parents can offer support and advice but ultimately let you decide how to handle it. This helps you build confidence in your ability to manage OCD on your own terms.

Managing parental stress is also important. Supporting a teen with OCD can be challenging, and parents need to take care of their own well-being to provide effective support. Practicing self-care and stress management techniques can help parents stay balanced and energized. Joining a support group for parents of teens with OCD can provide a sense of community and shared understanding. These groups offer a space to share experiences, ask questions, and learn from others who are in similar situations. If parents are feeling overwhelmed, seeking professional help can be beneficial. Talking to a therapist or counselor can provide them with strategies to manage their stress and support their teen more effectively.

Parents should also be aware of the importance of consistency in their approach. Being consistent in offering support, setting expectations, and respecting boundaries helps create a stable environment. For example, if parents agree to give you space to practice your coping strategies, they should stick to this agreement even when it's challenging. Inconsistent support can lead to confusion and increased anxiety. A consistent approach provides a sense of security and predictability, which can be incredibly comforting when dealing with OCD.

Encouraging open communication is another key aspect. Parents should create a safe space where you feel comfortable discussing your thoughts and feelings without fear of judgment. This means listening actively and empathetically, validating your experiences, and offering reassurance when needed. For example, if you're feeling anxious about an upcoming event, your parents can listen to your concerns, acknowledge your feelings, and offer suggestions on how to manage your anxiety. This kind of open, supportive communication can strengthen your relationship and make you feel more understood and supported.

In summary, parents can offer constructive support by encouraging you to take an active role in your treatment, providing guidance without being overly controlling, respecting your boundaries, and managing their own stress. This balanced approach helps foster independence while ensuring you feel supported and understood. By working together, you and your parents can create a supportive environment that makes managing OCD a little bit easier.

In the next chapter, we'll explore interactive exercises and journaling prompts designed to help you reflect on your progress, reduce anxiety, and enhance your problem-solving skills. These practical tools will help you foster self-awareness and resilience as you continue to manage your OCD.

INTERACTIVE EXERCISES AND
JOURNALING PROMPTS

❧

Let's say you've had a rough day. You're feeling overwhelmed, your mind is racing with thoughts, and the urge to perform compulsions is stronger than ever. What if there was a way to unload some of that mental clutter and make sense of your feelings? That's where journaling comes in. Think of journaling as a safe space where you can pour out your thoughts and emotions, without judgment or interruption. It's like having a conversation with yourself, helping you process what's going on in your mind and track your progress over time.

DAILY JOURNALING: REFLECTING ON YOUR PROGRESS

Journaling offers numerous benefits, especially if you're dealing with OCD. First, it provides an emotional release. When you write down your thoughts and feelings, you're essentially transferring some of your mental burden onto the paper. This act alone can reduce stress and make you feel lighter. According to Stanford Children's Health, journaling helps manage anxiety, reduce stress, and cope with depression by organizing thoughts and providing clarity. It's a way to vent your frustrations, celebrate your victories, and explore your feelings in a safe, private space.

In addition to emotional release, journaling enhances self-awareness. By regularly recording your thoughts, you start to notice patterns and triggers. For instance, you might find that your anxiety spikes every time you have a math test or when you're in crowded places. Recognizing these patterns can provide valuable insights into what triggers your OCD and how to manage it better. Over time, you'll develop a deeper understanding of yourself and your condition, empowering you to take proactive steps to manage your symptoms.

Getting started with daily journaling helps to have a few prompts to guide your reflections. These questions can spark introspection and help you focus on specific aspects of your day. For example, you might start with, "What were three positive things that happened today?" This question encourages you to look for the good moments, no matter how small, and shift your focus from negative to positive experiences. Another prompt could be, "What challenges did I face and how did I handle them?" This helps you reflect on difficult moments and recognize the coping strategies you used, reinforcing your ability to manage tough situations. Finally, consider asking yourself, "What is one thing I learned about myself today?" This prompt promotes self-discovery and personal growth, helping you uncover new insights about your strengths and areas for improvement.

Creating a consistent structure for your journal entries can make journaling a more effective and manageable habit. Start by noting the date and time of each entry. This provides a chronological record of your thoughts and experiences, making it easier to track your progress over time. Next, describe the events of your day and how you felt during each moment. Be honest and detailed in your descriptions; this will make your reflections more meaningful. After detailing your day, take a moment to reflect on the coping strategies you used. Did you practice deep breathing, engage in a hobby, or talk to a friend? Note what worked and what didn't, so you can refine your approach over time. To wrap up each entry, end with a positive affirmation. This could be something as simple as, "I am capable of managing my OCD," or "I am proud of my progress." Positive affirmations reinforce your strengths and provide a hopeful note to conclude your reflections.

Let's look at some sample journal entries to give you an idea of how to structure your own. Here's an example: "Today I felt anxious about my math test, but I used deep breathing to calm down. I learned that I can manage my anxiety with practice. Three positive things that happened today: I aced my English quiz, had a great conversation with my friend about our favorite books, and enjoyed a delicious lunch. Challenges: Felt overwhelmed during math class but handled it by focusing on my breathing. Positive affirmation: I am strong and capable." Another example might be: "Had a tough day with intrusive thoughts about contamination. I used mindfulness exercises to stay present and resist the urge to wash my hands. Learned that I'm stronger than I think. Positive events: Finished my homework on time, went for a relaxing walk, and had a fun movie night with my family. Challenges: Struggled with intrusive thoughts but managed to stay calm. Positive affirmation: I am in control of my actions."

By incorporating journaling into your daily routine, you can create a powerful tool for managing OCD. It helps you process your thoughts, track your progress, and gain valuable insights into your condition. Plus, it's a great way to practice self-compassion and celebrate your achievements, no matter how small. So grab a note-book or open a document on your computer, and start journaling today.

ANXIETY-REDUCTION EXERCISES: QUICK TECHNIQUES

Imagine you're sitting in class, and suddenly, your heart starts racing. Your palms get sweaty, and it feels like you can't catch your breath. Anxiety can hit hard and fast, making it difficult to focus on anything else. In moments like these, having quick, effective tech-niques to reduce anxiety can be a game-changer. One of the simplest and most effective methods is deep breathing. The 4-7-8 technique is a great place to start. To practice this, sit comfortably and close your eyes. Breathe in through your nose for a count of four. Hold your breath for a count of seven. Then, exhale completely through your mouth for a count of eight. Repeat this cycle a few times. This technique helps regulate oxygen and carbon dioxide levels in your body, promoting relaxation and clearer thoughts.

Another helpful exercise is Progressive Muscle Relaxation, or PMR. This technique focuses on tensing and then relaxing each muscle group in your body. Start by finding a quiet place where you can sit or lie down comfortably. Begin with your toes, tensing the muscles for about ten seconds and then slowly releasing the tension. Move up to your calves, thighs, and so on, until you've worked through each muscle group. This practice helps your brain recog-nize the difference between tension and relaxation, reducing uncon-scious tension that can trigger anxiety. By focusing on your body, you also divert your mind from anxious thoughts, giving yourself a much-needed break.

Grounding techniques are another fantastic way to stay present and manage anxiety. The 5-4-3-2-1 sensory exercise is simple yet effective. Start by naming five things you can see around you. Then, focus on four things you can touch. Next, identify three things you can hear, two things you can smell, and one thing you can taste. This exercise engages all your senses, bringing you fully into the present moment. If you find it challenging to concentrate during an anxiety episode, try using a grounding object like a stress ball or a piece of jewelry. Holding and focusing on this object can help anchor you to the here and now, reducing the intensity of your anxiety.

Visualization exercises can also be incredibly calming. Imagine a place where you feel completely relaxed and safe. This could be a beach with gentle waves lapping at the shore, a peaceful forest with the sound of birds chirping, or even a cozy room with a warm fire. Close your eyes and picture yourself in this place. Focus on the details—the sound of the waves, the smell of the forest, the warmth of the fire. Guided imagery scripts can help you through this process, providing a structured way to visualize and relax. You can find these scripts online or even record your own, tailoring them to what makes you feel most at peace.

Physical activity is another effective way to reduce anxiety quickly. Short, brisk walks can work wonders. Stepping outside for a few minutes, focusing on the rhythm of your steps, and taking in your surroundings can help clear your mind and reduce stress. Pay attention to the feel of the ground beneath your feet, the sound of birds, or the rustling of leaves. This simple exercise not only provides a physical outlet for your anxiety but also engages your senses, grounding you in the present moment. Stretching or practicing yoga poses can also be beneficial. Try the "child's pose," which involves kneeling on the floor, sitting back on your heels, and stretching your arms forward while resting your forehead on the ground. This position is incredibly soothing and can help release tension in your body.

Incorporating these techniques into your daily routine can help you manage anxiety more effectively. Whether you're in class, at home, or out with friends, having these tools at your disposal can make a significant difference. Experiment with different exercises to find what works best for you. The more you practice, the easier it will become to use these techniques whenever anxiety starts to creep in. Remember, you have the power to take control of your anxiety and find moments of calm amidst the chaos.

THOUGHT RECORDS: TRACKING AND CHALLENGING YOUR THOUGHTS

Imagine you're sitting in your room, feeling a wave of anxiety wash over you because of an intrusive thought. It tells you that something terrible will happen if you don't check the door lock again. You know it's irrational, but the anxiety is overwhelming. This is where thought records come in handy. They help you track and challenge these negative thoughts, making them less powerful over time. Thought records are tools that help you identify automatic negative thoughts, understand how these thoughts affect your feelings and behaviors, and learn to challenge and reframe them. By regularly using thought records, you can start to see patterns in your thinking and recognize the triggers that set off your OCD symptoms.

A thought record usually follows a structured format, making it easier to analyze and challenge your thoughts. Start with the situation: describe the triggering event that caused the negative thought. For example, you might write, "I was getting ready for bed and thought I hadn't locked the front door." Next, identify the negative thoughts that popped into your mind. This could be, "If I don't check the lock, someone will break in." Then, note the emotions you felt in response to this thought—maybe you felt anxious, scared, or uneasy. The next step is to challenge the thought by questioning its validity. Ask yourself, "What evidence do I have for and against this thought?" Finally, replace the negative thought with a more balanced one. For instance, "I always lock the door before bed. It's unlikely that it's unlocked now."

Challenging negative thoughts can feel daunting, but it gets easier with practice. One effective strategy is to ask yourself questions that help reframe the thought. For example, "What evidence do I have for and against this thought?" If you're worried about the door being unlocked, think back to all the times you've checked it before and found it locked. Another helpful question is, "Is there another way to look at this situation?" Instead of thinking, "I must check the lock," consider, "I can trust that I locked the door and focus on getting a good night's sleep." Replacing negative thoughts with more balanced ones can significantly reduce the anxiety they cause. Instead of thinking, "I'm a failure," reframe it to, "I'm learning and growing."

To illustrate how thought records work, let's look at some examples. Imagine you failed a test and your automatic thought is, "I'm not smart enough." This thought makes you feel sad and anxious. When you challenge it, you realize you've passed other tests before and that one failed test doesn't define your intelligence. The alternative thought could be, "This is one test, and I can improve with practice." Another example might be an argument with a friend. Your negative thought is, "They hate me," which makes you feel hurt and rejected. When you challenge this thought, you remember that you've had disagreements before and made up. The alternative thought could be, "We can talk it out and resolve this."

Using thought records regularly can help you gain control over your negative thoughts and reduce their impact on your life. They provide a structured way to analyze and reframe your thoughts, making it easier to manage OCD symptoms. By identifying patterns and triggers, you can take proactive steps to challenge and change your thinking, leading to a more balanced and less anxious mindset.

REFLECTIVE ACTIVITIES: DEEPENING YOUR UNDERSTANDING

Reflective activities can be a powerful way to gain deeper insights into your thoughts and behaviors. They encourage self-exploration and personal growth, allowing you to understand yourself better and enhance your emotional intelligence. By taking time to reflect, you can identify patterns in your thoughts and behaviors, recognize your strengths, and find areas where you can improve. For example, reflecting on significant life events can reveal how these experiences have shaped your values and beliefs. This kind of introspection helps you understand why you think and act the way you do, making it easier to manage your OCD symptoms.

One effective reflective activity is writing a letter to your future self. This exercise allows you to articulate your hopes and dreams, as well as your current struggles and achievements. Start your letter with something like, "Dear Future Me, I hope you have found peace and happiness..." This exercise not only helps you set goals but also provides a snapshot of your current mindset, which can be insightful when you read it later. Another powerful exercise is reflecting on your personal strengths and achievements. List five strengths and think about how they have helped you in difficult situations. For example, if you consider yourself resilient, reflect on a time when this trait helped you overcome a challenging experience.

Recognizing your strengths can boost your confidence and motivate you to keep pushing forward.

Creative reflection methods can make the process more engaging and enjoyable. Drawing or painting your feelings is a great way to express emotions that might be hard to put into words. Create an art piece that represents your journey with OCD. This could be as abstract or detailed as you like. Perhaps you draw a stormy sea to represent the turbulence you feel, with a sturdy ship sailing through it to symbolize your resilience. Using music or poetry to express your emotions is another creative outlet. Write a poem or song that captures your feelings and experiences. These creative methods can provide a fresh perspective and make reflection feel less like a chore and more like an enjoyable activity.

To guide your reflective practice, consider using thought-provoking questions. These can help you dig deeper into your experiences and gain more meaningful insights. Ask yourself, "What have I learned about myself through my struggles with OCD?" This question encourages you to see your challenges as opportunities for growth. Another question might be, "How have my experiences shaped my values and beliefs?" Reflecting on this can help you understand what truly matters to you and why. Finally, ask yourself, "What steps can I take to continue growing and improving?" This prompts you to think proactively about your personal development and set goals for the future.

Reflective activities help you explore your thoughts and behaviors, enhancing self-awareness and emotional intelligence. They allow you to understand yourself better, recognize patterns in your thinking, and identify areas for growth. By engaging in exercises like writing a letter to your future self, reflecting on your strengths, and using creative methods like drawing or music, you can make the process enjoyable and insightful. Thought-provoking questions guide your reflections, helping you gain deeper insights and set goals for continued personal development.

In the next chapter, we'll explore how managing stress and identifying triggers play a crucial role in handling OCD. You'll learn practical strategies to stay calm and focused, making it easier to navigate daily life.

MANAGING STRESS AND TRIGGERS

❧

I magine you're sitting in class, trying to focus on the lesson, but your mind is somewhere else entirely. You can't stop thinking about the mess in your locker or the germs on your desk. You feel this overwhelming urge to do something about it, but you're stuck. You start tapping your foot, biting your nails, or zoning out completely. Sound familiar? This is how stress and triggers can affect you when you have OCD. Understanding these triggers is a crucial step in managing your symptoms effectively.

IDENTIFYING YOUR TRIGGERS: SELF-DISCOVERY TOOLS

Recognizing specific stressors is like having a flashlight in a dark room. It helps you see where you're going and avoid bumping into things. When you know what sets off your OCD, you can prepare yourself better and use strategies to manage these situations. Stress and OCD are closely linked. When you're stressed, your OCD symptoms can become more intense. It's like pouring gasoline on a fire. Understanding your triggers can help you reduce stress and, in turn, lessen OCD flare-ups.

One of the most effective ways to identify your triggers is through journaling. Keep a daily log of your activities and emotional responses. Write down what you were doing, how you felt, and any compulsive behaviors you engaged in. Over time, you'll start to see patterns. For example, you might notice that social gatherings make you anxious, leading to more compulsive behaviors. Seeing these patterns can be eye-opening and empowering. You'll realize that certain situations consistently trigger your OCD, giving you a starting point for managing these triggers.

Another helpful tool is a trigger tracking worksheet. This is a structured way to document your triggers and responses. Each time you feel the urge to perform a compulsion, note down the situation, your thoughts, and your actions. For instance, if you feel the need to wash your hands after touching a doorknob, write it down. Over time, you'll build a comprehensive list of your triggers. This list will be invaluable in helping you develop strategies to manage your OCD more effectively.

Common triggers for teens with OCD often revolve around academic pressures, social interactions, and family dynamics. Think about the stress of exams and homework. The pressure to do well can be overwhelming, leading to intrusive thoughts about failure or not being good enough. Social interactions can also be a major trigger. Peer pressure, public speaking, or just trying to fit in can cause significant anxiety. Family dynamics, like conflicts or high expectations, can add another layer of stress, exacerbating your OCD symptoms.

To help you reflect on your triggers, try mind mapping. Start with a central theme, like "school," and branch out to specific triggers like "tests" and "presentations." This visual approach can make it easier to see the connections between different stressors and how they impact your OCD. Another effective exercise is reflective journaling. Use prompts focused on identifying stress points, such as "What situations made me feel anxious today?" or "When did I feel the urge to perform a compulsion?" Writing about these experiences can increase self-awareness and help you understand your triggers better.

Mind mapping is a great way to visualize the connections between different stressors and OCD symptoms. For example, start with "school" in the center of your mind map. Branch out to specific triggers like "tests," "homework," "group projects," and "public speaking." Under each of these, list how they make you feel and the compulsions they trigger. This exercise can help you see the bigger picture and identify common themes in your triggers. It's like connecting the dots, giving you a clearer understanding of what sets off your OCD.

Reflective journaling prompts can guide you in identifying your stress points. Here are a few to get you started: "What situations made me feel anxious today?" "When did I feel the urge to perform a compulsion?" "What thoughts were going through my mind when I felt stressed?" "How did I respond to these thoughts and feelings?" Writing about these experiences can increase your self-awareness and help you understand your triggers better. It's like having a conversation with yourself, helping you make sense of your emotions and reactions.

Understanding your triggers is the first step in managing your OCD more effectively. By keeping a journal, using trigger tracking worksheets, and engaging in reflective exercises like mind mapping and journaling, you can identify the specific stressors that exacerbate your symptoms. This self-awareness is empowering. It gives you the tools you need to anticipate and manage your triggers, reducing their impact on your daily life. Recognize your triggers, understand them, and take control of your OCD.

STRESS MANAGEMENT TECHNIQUES: FINDING WHAT WORKS FOR YOU

Managing stress is like finding the right pair of shoes. What works for one person might not work for another. That's why it's important to explore different stress management techniques to see what fits best for you. Physical activities can be a great way to channel your energy and reduce stress. Exercise, whether it's running, swimming, or even a brisk walk, releases endorphins, which are natural mood lifters. Yoga combines physical movement with mindfulness, helping you stay present and calm. Creative outlets like drawing, painting, or playing music allow you to express your emotions in a healthy way, providing a break from your worries.

Relaxation practices such as meditation and deep breathing can also be incredibly effective. Meditation helps you focus on the present moment, reducing anxiety about the past or future. Deep breathing exercises, like the 4-7-8 technique, can quickly calm your nervous system. Imagine sitting in a quiet room, focusing solely on your breath. Inhale for four seconds, hold for seven, and exhale for eight. This simple act can make a world of difference when you're feeling overwhelmed.

Experimentation is key to finding what works best for you. Try various activities and note their effects. For example, you might find that running helps clear your mind, while painting allows you to express your feelings more freely. Keeping a stress management journal can help you track the effectiveness of different techniques. Write down what you tried, how you felt before and after, and any changes in your stress levels or OCD symptoms. This will give you a clearer picture of what's most beneficial for you.

Integrating stress management into your daily routine is crucial. It's not enough to use these techniques only when you're already stressed; making them a regular part of your life can prevent stress from building up in the first place. Set aside specific times for relaxation activities. For example, allocate ten minutes each morning for deep breathing exercises. This can set a calm tone for the day ahead. Create a balanced schedule that includes time for leisure and self-care. Whether it's reading a book, taking a bath, or spending time with friends, make sure you have activities that bring you joy and relaxation.

Managing stress in different settings requires tailored strategies. At school, techniques for reducing test anxiety can be a lifesaver. Practice visualization before exams. Close your eyes and picture yourself confidently answering questions and finishing on time. This mental rehearsal can reduce anxiety and improve performance. When dealing with family conflicts, effective communication is key. Use "I" statements to express your feelings without blaming others. For example, say, "I feel stressed when there's a lot of noise during my study time," instead of, "You're always making too much noise." This approach can help you communicate more effectively and reduce tension.

Finding what works for you might take some time, but it's worth the effort. Each person is different, and what brings relief to one might not work for another. Keep experimenting, stay consistent, and remember that managing stress is a continuous process. With the right techniques, you can create a more balanced, less stressful life.

BUILDING RESILIENCE: COPING WITH DAILY CHALLENGES

Resilience is like a rubber band. It's the ability to stretch and bend without breaking, to bounce back after being pulled in all directions. When you have OCD, resilience becomes your secret weapon. It helps you cope with the daily challenges and stressors that come your way. Resilience is crucial because it allows you to view setbacks as opportunities for growth rather than defeats. Imagine you've had a tough day, and your OCD symptoms are flaring up. Instead of feeling defeated, resilience helps you see this as a chance to practice your coping strategies and come out stronger.

Developing resilience isn't something that happens overnight, but it can definitely be strengthened with practice. Start by cultivating a positive mindset. This doesn't mean ignoring your struggles or pretending everything is okay. It means focusing on the good things in your life, no matter how small. One way to do this is by practicing gratitude. Each day, take a moment to list three things you're thankful for. They can be as simple as enjoying a sunny day, having a supportive friend, or finishing a difficult task. This practice can shift your focus from what's going wrong to what's going right, helping you build a more positive outlook.

Building strong support networks is another key aspect of resilience. Surround yourself with people who understand and support you. This could be family, friends, or even a support group for teens with OCD. Having a network of people you can turn to for advice, encouragement, or just a listening ear can make a world of difference. For example, joining a support group can provide a sense of community and shared understanding. You'll realize you're not alone in your struggles, and you can learn from others who are going through similar experiences.

Self-compassion plays a huge role in resilience. Being kind to yourself during difficult times can make it easier to bounce back. Practice positive self-talk. Instead of criticizing yourself for your struggles, acknowledge your efforts and remind yourself that it's okay to have tough days. Write a compassionate letter to yourself when you're having a hard time. Imagine you're writing to a friend who is going through the same struggles. What would you say to them? How would you comfort and encourage them? Write these words to yourself. This exercise can help you develop a kinder, more supportive inner dialogue.

To build resilience, engage in exercises that strengthen your ability to cope with challenges. Reflective journaling is a powerful tool. Write about past challenges and how you overcame them. For instance, think about a time when you faced a fear and succeeded. Maybe it was giving a presentation despite your anxiety or resisting a compulsion for the first time. Reflecting on these victories can remind you of your strength and resilience. Visualization exercises can also be helpful. Close your eyes and imagine handling future stressors with confidence. Picture yourself using your coping strategies effectively and coming out the other side stronger. Visualization can boost your confidence and prepare you for real-life challenges.

Resilience is a skill you can develop and strengthen over time. It's about learning to view setbacks as opportunities for growth, cultivating a positive mindset, building strong support networks, and practicing self-compassion. By engaging in exercises like reflective journaling and visualization, you can enhance your resilience and better cope with the daily challenges of OCD.

RELAXATION TECHNIQUES: FINDING CALM IN CHAOS

Imagine getting home after a long day at school. Your mind is buzzing with thoughts about all the things you need to do and the intrusive thoughts that have been nagging at you all day. You feel tense, anxious, and exhausted. This is where relaxation techniques come in. They can help you find calm amidst the chaos, reducing stress and improving your overall well-being. Regular relaxation practices are like a balm for both your mind and body. They not only help you unwind but also play a crucial role in managing OCD symptoms. When you practice relaxation techniques consistently, you might notice a reduction in the frequency and intensity of intrusive thoughts.

One effective relaxation technique is progressive muscle relaxation (PMR). This practice involves tensing and then relaxing each muscle group in your body, starting from your toes and moving up to your head. For instance, begin by curling your toes tightly for a few seconds, then release and feel the tension melt away. Move on to your calves, thighs, and so on until you've relaxed every part of your body. This method helps you become more aware of physical tension and teaches you how to release it, which can be incredibly soothing when you're feeling overwhelmed.

Guided imagery and visualization are also powerful tools. Close your eyes and imagine yourself in a peaceful place—maybe a serene beach with waves gently crashing, or a quiet forest with birds chirping. Picture the scene in as much detail as possible: the colors, sounds, smells, and textures. This mental escape can transport you away from your worries and create a sense of calm. Visualization can be especially helpful during moments of high anxiety, providing a mental refuge where you can regroup and relax.

Mindfulness meditation is another technique that can help you stay present and reduce anxiety. Find a quiet spot and focus on your breath. Breathe in slowly through your nose, hold for a few seconds, and then exhale through your mouth. As you breathe, observe your thoughts without judgment. Imagine them as leaves floating down a stream—acknowledge their presence but let them drift away. This practice helps you detach from intrusive thoughts and reduces their power over you. It's like training your mind to stay calm and centered, even when faced with stress.

Creating a relaxing environment at home is essential for making these practices effective. Set up a space that's conducive to relaxation. Dim the lights, play some soothing music, and choose comfortable seating. Consider creating a "relaxation corner" with cushions, blankets, and sensory items like scented candles or essential oils. This designated space can become your go-to spot for unwinding, making it easier to incorporate relaxation into your daily routine. The environment you create can significantly enhance the effectiveness of your relaxation practices, making them more enjoyable and beneficial.

Incorporating relaxation into your daily life doesn't have to be complicated. Start by scheduling relaxation breaks throughout your day. For instance, take a five-minute mindfulness break between classes. Find a quiet spot, close your eyes, and focus on your breath. This short pause can help reset your mind and reduce stress. You can also combine relaxation techniques with other activities. For example, practice deep breathing while listening to calming music or stretch before bed to help your body and mind unwind. These small, consistent practices can add up, creating a more relaxed and balanced daily routine.

Regular relaxation practices can significantly reduce stress and improve your overall well-being. Techniques like progressive muscle relaxation, guided imagery, and mindfulness meditation can help you manage OCD symptoms by reducing the frequency of intrusive thoughts. Creating a calming environment and incorporating relaxation into your daily routine can make these techniques more effective. By finding what works best for you and making relaxation a regular habit, you can navigate the challenges of OCD with greater ease and resilience.

LONG-TERM STRATEGIES FOR LIVING WELL WITH OCD

Imagine climbing a mountain. You've made it past the steepest parts, but the journey isn't over. You need to keep moving, one step at a time, to reach the summit. Managing OCD is a lot like this. You've worked hard to get where you are, and maintaining that progress is crucial. Slowing down or stopping can lead to setbacks, but if you keep up the momentum, the view from the top is worth it.

MAINTAINING YOUR GAINS: KEEPING THE MOMENTUM

Keeping the momentum you've built in managing your OCD is essential for long-term success. You've already made significant progress, and it's important to prevent any regression. Think of it like building a sandcastle; if you stop adding to it and reinforcing the walls, the tide can wash it away. The same goes for your OCD management. Regularly practicing coping strategies helps reinforce the new habits you've developed, making them second nature over time. This consistency builds a solid foundation that can withstand the challenges you might face.

One practical way to maintain your gains is by regularly reviewing and updating your goals. Set aside time each month to assess your progress and make any necessary adjustments. This could be as simple as writing down what you've achieved and what you still want to work on. For example, if you've been practicing mindfulness daily and notice a positive change, you might decide to increase your practice time or add another coping strategy to your routine. These monthly check-ins keep you on track and ensure you're continuously moving forward.

Continuing with therapy or support groups is another effective strategy for maintaining progress. Regular sessions with a therapist can provide ongoing support and guidance, helping you navigate any new challenges that arise. Support groups offer a sense of community and understanding, where you can share experiences and learn from others. Participating in bi-weekly group therapy sessions, for instance, can be incredibly beneficial. These sessions not only reinforce what you've learned but also provide a space to discuss any setbacks and find collective solutions.

Consistency is key when it comes to managing OCD. Regular practice and adherence to routines are vital for long-term success. Incorporate OCD management techniques into your daily life, such as mindfulness practice or ERP exercises. For example, make it a habit to start your day with a short mindfulness session, focusing on your breath and setting a positive tone for the day. Integrating these practices into your routine ensures that they become a natural part of your life, rather than something you have to remind yourself to do.

Staying motivated is essential to keep the momentum going. Celebrate your small successes to maintain high motivation and prevent burnout. Reward yourself after a month of consistent progress. This could be something simple like treating yourself to your favorite snack or spending extra time on a hobby you enjoy. Recognizing and celebrating your achievements, no matter how small, can boost your confidence and encourage you to keep going.

Finding inspiration from others can also help you stay motivated. Reading success stories or joining online forums where people share their experiences can provide a sense of solidarity and encouragement. Knowing that others have faced similar challenges and overcome them can give you the strength to continue your journey. You might discover new strategies or perspectives that resonate with you, adding to your toolbox of coping mechanisms.

By maintaining your gains, regularly reviewing your goals, continuing with therapy or support groups, practicing consistency, and staying motivated, you can ensure long-term success in managing your OCD. Remember, every small step you take brings you closer to living a life where OCD doesn't hold you back. Keep moving forward, and you'll find that the view from the top is truly worth it.

RELAPSE PREVENTION: RECOGNIZING AND ADDRESSING SETBACKS

Setbacks are a normal part of managing OCD, and it's important to understand that they don't mean you've failed. Everyone experiences bumps in the road, and recognizing this can help you approach setbacks with a healthier mindset. Imagine you're studying for an exam, and you miss a couple of study sessions. It doesn't mean you've failed the exam; it just means you need to get back on track. The same goes for OCD. Recognizing early warning signs of a potential relapse, like increased anxiety or returning compulsions, can help you address them before they become overwhelming.

To minimize the risk of setbacks, maintaining regular therapy sessions is crucial. Think of therapy as a maintenance check for your mental health. Scheduling monthly check-ins with a therapist can help you stay on top of your progress and address any emerging issues. Even if you feel like you're doing well, these sessions can provide valuable support and prevent small issues from becoming bigger problems.

Continuing to use coping strategies daily is another effective way to prevent setbacks. Practicing ERP even when your symptoms are minimal can keep your skills sharp and ready for use when needed. It's like exercising regularly to stay in shape; the more consistent you are, the better equipped you'll be to handle challenges. Keeping a log of recent stressors and OCD symptoms can help you identify patterns and triggers. This awareness allows you to proactively address potential setbacks and adjust your coping strategies accordingly.

If a setback does occur, it's important to respond effectively. Start by identifying the triggers and stressors that contributed to the relapse. Keeping a log can help you pinpoint these factors. Once you understand what triggered the setback, re-engage with your therapeutic techniques. Revisit ERP exercises or mindfulness practices that have worked for you in the past. These techniques are tools in your toolkit, ready to be used whenever needed.

Emma experienced a setback during exam season. The stress of exams triggered her compulsions, and she found herself returning to old habits. Recognizing the signs early, she re-engaged with her therapist and focused on her ERP exercises. She also practiced mindfulness to manage her stress. Jake faced a setback after a family conflict. The emotional turmoil caused his intrusive thoughts to spike. He kept a log of his stressors, which helped him understand the connection between the conflict and his symptoms. By revisiting his coping strategies and seeking support from his therapist, Jake regained control.

BUILDING A SUPPORT NETWORK: FRIENDS, FAMILY, AND PROFESSIONALS

Having a strong support network is like having a safety net. Friends, family, and professionals can provide both emotional and practical support, giving you the encouragement and accountability you need to manage your OCD. Imagine having a friend who checks in on you regularly, asking how you're doing and listening to your challenges. This kind of support can make a big difference. Your family can also play a crucial role. When they understand what you're going through, they can offer more empathy and less judgment. Professionals, like therapists, bring expertise that can guide you through tough times and provide strategies tailored to your needs.

Building and maintaining a support network starts with open communication. Talking to friends and family about your progress and challenges can help them understand your situation better. Share your experiences and let them know how they can support you. For instance, you might tell a trusted family member about a recent breakthrough in therapy or a new coping strategy you're trying. This openness fosters understanding and strengthens your relationships. Seeking professional support when needed is also important. Finding a therapist who specializes in OCD can provide you with specific techniques and insights that general therapy might not cover. Regular sessions with a specialist can help you stay on track and tackle any new issues that arise.

Support groups offer a sense of community and understanding that can be incredibly uplifting. Joining a group for teens with OCD allows you to share experiences and coping strategies in a safe, non-judgmental environment. Attending weekly meetings can provide a consistent source of support and motivation. These groups can be both in-person and online, making them accessible no matter where you are. Sharing your journey with others who understand what you're going through can reduce feelings of isolation and provide new perspectives on managing OCD.

To strengthen your support network, consider activities that build and maintain strong connections. Writing a letter of appreciation to a supportive friend or family member can deepen your bond. Expressing gratitude for their encouragement and support not only makes them feel valued but also reinforces the positive aspects of your relationship. Planning regular meetups or check-ins with your support network members keeps these relationships active and meaningful. Whether it's a weekly coffee date with a friend or a monthly family dinner, these regular interactions provide ongoing support and help maintain strong connections.

PLANNING FOR THE FUTURE: SETTING NEW GOALS

Setting new goals is like mapping out your next adventure. It gives you direction and motivation, helping you focus on continuous personal growth. Imagine setting a goal to excel in your favorite subject or to pursue a new hobby. These goals not only push you to improve but also build a sense of purpose and direction in your life. When you have something to strive for, it makes each day more meaningful.

To start setting long-term goals, identify areas where you want to grow and improve. Maybe you want to learn a new skill, like playing a musical instrument, or perhaps you're aiming for academic achievements. Break these long-term goals into manageable steps. For instance, if your goal is to learn guitar, start by setting a timeline for each milestone—like learning basic chords in the first month, playing simple songs in the next, and so on. This approach makes big goals feel less overwhelming and more achievable.

Creating a vision board can be a fun and motivating way to visualize your goals. Gather images, quotes, and anything that represents your future aspirations. Arrange them on a board or in a digital format where you can see them daily. This visual reminder keeps you focused and inspired. Another practical tool is a goal-setting worksheet. Write down your specific, measurable, achievable, relevant, and time-bound (SMART) goals. For example, "I will practice guitar for 30 minutes every day for the next three months." This clarity helps you stay on track and measure your progress.

Regularly reviewing and adjusting your goals is crucial. Set monthly check-ins to assess how far you've come and what needs tweaking. Life is dynamic, and your goals should be flexible to accommodate changes. Maybe a new opportunity arises, or perhaps you realize that a goal needs more time. Adjusting your goals based on these circumstances ensures they remain relevant and attainable.

As you work towards your goals, remember to keep an open mind and be patient with yourself. Progress might be slow at times, but consistency pays off. Every small step brings you closer to your aspirations, and with each achievement, you'll find a renewed sense of purpose and motivation.

EMBRACING YOUR JOURNEY: CELEBRATING YOUR PROGRESS

Think about the last time you achieved something significant, no matter how small. Maybe you finally completed a challenging school project or went a week without giving in to a compulsion. Celebrating these moments is crucial for your long-term success. Recognizing your achievements boosts your self-esteem and motivation, reinforcing the positive behaviors and habits you've worked hard to develop. Imagine celebrating milestones with your friends and family. Their encouragement can make you feel proud and more determined to keep going.

There are many meaningful ways to celebrate your progress. Planning a special outing or activity can be a fantastic reward. Consider going on a day trip to a favorite place—maybe a beach, a hiking trail, or a city you've always wanted to explore. Treating yourself to something you desire is another great idea. Perhaps there's a book you've been eyeing, or a concert you'd love to attend. These treats serve as tangible reminders of your hard work and dedication, making the journey feel worthwhile.

Reflecting on your progress is equally important. Take some time to look back on where you started and how far you've come. Write a reflection on your accomplishments and the challenges you've overcome. Creating a scrapbook or journal entry highlighting key milestones can be a fun and rewarding way to document your journey. Sharing your story with others can also be empowering. Whether it's through a blog, social media, or a conversation with a friend, sharing your experiences can inspire others and remind you of your resilience.

Engaging in exercises for self-reflection and celebration can deepen your self-awareness and appreciation for your progress. Try writing a letter to your past self, reflecting on the lessons learned and the growth you've experienced. This exercise can be incredibly powerful, helping you see the strength and determination that have carried you through tough times. Another idea is creating a "success time-line." Map out significant achievements and turning points in your journey. Seeing your progress visually can be motivating and provide a clear picture of how much you've accomplished.

Embracing your journey and celebrating your progress is about acknowledging the hard work you've put in and the growth you've achieved. It's about taking a moment to appreciate yourself and the strides you've made. So go ahead, plan that outing, treat yourself, and take time to reflect. You've earned it.

FINDING YOUR PASSION: PURSUING HOBBIES AND INTERESTS

Imagine having something you look forward to every day, something that brings you joy and makes you forget about the stresses of life. That's the magic of hobbies and interests. Engaging in meaningful activities provides a sense of fulfillment and purpose, which can significantly improve your mental health and well-being. Imagine losing yourself in a painting, where each brushstroke calms your mind, or strumming a guitar and feeling the music flow through you. These creative pursuits not only reduce stress and anxiety but also offer a productive outlet for your emotions.

Exploring new hobbies and interests is like opening a treasure chest of possibilities. You might not know what you're passionate about until you try different things. Think about joining a local club or taking a workshop that piques your interest. Whether it's pottery, coding, or dance, trying out new activities can be exciting and eye-opening. Set aside time in your daily routine to explore these interests. Scheduling regular time for a favorite activity, like dedicating Saturday afternoons to photography, can help you stay committed and make these hobbies a consistent part of your life.

Balancing hobbies with other responsibilities might seem challenging, but it's all about prioritizing what brings you joy and fulfillment. Allocate specific days or times for hobby activities, ensuring they fit into your schedule without overwhelming you. For example, you might decide that Tuesdays and Thursdays are your painting days. Creating a balanced schedule that includes leisure and self-care is crucial. It's not just about fitting hobbies into your life; it's about making time for activities that help you recharge and stay grounded.

Emma found peace through gardening. She discovered that tending to plants provided a soothing escape from her intrusive thoughts. The act of nurturing something and watching it grow gave her a sense of accomplishment and tranquility. Jake, on the other hand, discovered a love for photography. Capturing moments through his lens allowed him to see the world differently and provided a creative outlet for his emotions. These activities helped them manage their OCD by offering a break from their routines and a way to channel their energy positively.

Finding your passion can be a transformative experience. It's about discovering what makes you tick and integrating it into your life. So, go ahead and explore new hobbies, balance them with your responsibilities, and see how they can positively impact your well-being.

ADVOCACY AND AWARENESS: SHARING YOUR STORY TO HELP OTHERS

Imagine standing in front of your school assembly and sharing your personal experience with OCD. It might sound nerve-wracking, but it can be incredibly powerful. When you speak openly about your struggles and triumphs, you reduce the stigma surrounding OCD and help others understand it better. Your story can provide hope and inspiration to those who might be facing similar challenges but feel alone. Sharing personal experiences helps normalize the condition and encourages others to seek help.

There are many ways you can advocate and raise awareness. Writing blog posts or articles about your journey can reach a wide audience. Share your experiences on a mental health website, where others can read your story and find solace in knowing they're not alone. Speaking at events or participating in awareness campaigns is another impactful way to spread the word. Imagine joining a local or national OCD awareness event, where you can connect with others and share your insights. These platforms provide an opportunity to educate and inspire those who might be struggling in silence.

Effective storytelling is all about being honest and vulnerable. When you describe your personal struggles and triumphs authentically, you create a connection with your audience. Use specific examples and anecdotes to highlight key moments and lessons learned. For instance, talk about a particularly challenging day and how you managed to overcome it. This approach makes your story relatable and impactful, helping others see that they too can navigate their challenges.

To develop your advocacy skills, start by writing a draft of your personal story. Outline significant events and insights that you want to share. Practice public speaking or presentation skills with a friend or family member. Rehearse your speech or presentation until you feel comfortable and confident. This practice helps you refine your message and delivery, making it more compelling.

Sharing your story is not just about helping others; it's also about empowering yourself. When you speak up, you reclaim your narrative and take control of your experience. So, whether it's through writing, speaking, or participating in campaigns, your voice matters. Your story has the power to change lives, including your own.

LIVING A BALANCED LIFE: INTEGRATING OCD MANAGEMENT INTO YOUR DAILY ROUTINE

Finding balance in your daily life is crucial when managing OCD. Integrating OCD management techniques into your routine helps reduce the impact of symptoms on your daily activities and promotes overall well-being. Imagine your day as a pie chart, with each slice representing different activities. A balanced schedule includes time for school, hobbies, self-care, and relaxation. This balance ensures that OCD doesn't dominate your life, allowing you to enjoy various aspects of your day.

To integrate OCD management into your daily routine, start by scheduling regular practice of coping strategies. Allocate specific times each day for mindfulness or ERP exercises. For example, you might set aside 15 minutes in the morning for mindfulness meditation and another 15 minutes in the evening for ERP exercises. This regular practice helps reinforce the techniques you've learned and makes them a natural part of your day.

Balancing responsibilities with leisure and self-care is also essential. Ensure you dedicate time for hobbies and relaxation alongside your schoolwork. For instance, after completing your homework, take a break to engage in a favorite activity like drawing or playing a sport. This balance prevents burnout and keeps you motivated. Remember, it's important to make time for activities that bring you joy and help you unwind.

Developing healthy habits is another key component of a balanced life. Establish consistent sleep patterns by creating a bedtime routine that promotes better sleep quality. This might include turning off screens an hour before bed, reading a book, or practicing deep breathing exercises. Maintaining a healthy diet and regular exercise also supports mental health. Plan balanced meals that include a variety of nutrients and incorporate physical activity into your day. Even a short walk after dinner can make a difference.

Flexibility and adaptability in your routines are important. Adjust your routines based on changing circumstances. For example, during busy school periods, you might need to modify your exercise plans. Instead of a long workout, opt for shorter, more intense sessions. Being open to trying new strategies and approaches can also help you find what works best for you. Experiment with different relaxation techniques to discover which ones are most effective in managing your stress and OCD symptoms.

Incorporating OCD management into your daily routine promotes a balanced life, reducing the impact of symptoms and enhancing overall well-being. Balancing responsibilities with self-care, developing healthy habits, and staying flexible in your routines are all part of living well with OCD. Keep these strategies in mind as you navigate your daily life, and remember that finding balance is an ongoing process that evolves with your needs and circumstances.

As you continue to manage your OCD, consider how these strategies can be applied to other areas of your life. In the next chapter, we'll explore the importance of building a supportive community and how connecting with others can enhance your journey toward well-being.

CONCLUSION

Wow, what a journey we've taken together! From the very first page, where we delved into understanding OCD and its impact on your life, to mastering long-term strategies for managing it, you've come a long way. We've explored the depths of your mind, tackled those pesky intrusive thoughts, and developed practical tools to help you reclaim control over your life.

Remember when we started with the basics of OCD? We learned about obsessions and compulsions, and how they can turn everyday activities into a battlefield of anxious thoughts and repetitive actions. But you didn't stop there. You learned about different therapeutic techniques like CBT, DBT, ACT, and the Triple-A Response®. Each of these methods provided you with powerful strategies to challenge and change those negative thought patterns.

You didn't shy away from the tough stuff. You faced your fears head-on through Exposure and Response Prevention (ERP). You embraced mindfulness and meditation practices to find peace amidst the chaos. You set SMART goals to track your progress and build confidence. You even explored the importance of exercise and nutrition for your mental health.

Let's not forget the real-life case studies. Emma, Jake, Lily, and Alex showed you that you're not alone. Their stories of overcoming school anxiety, managing social fears, balancing OCD with sports, and building supportive friendships were sources of inspiration and motivation.

We also dove into the crucial role of family support. Educating your family about OCD, encouraging open discussions, and involving them in your treatment plan can make a world of difference. Building a supportive home environment and effective communication are key to creating a space where you can thrive.

Then came the interactive exercises and journaling prompts. These tools helped you reflect on your progress, reduce anxiety, and enhance your problem-solving skills. You learned the importance of daily journaling, anxiety-reduction techniques, thought records, and reflective activities. Each exercise was designed to foster self-awareness and resilience.

Managing stress and triggers became another essential part of your toolkit. Identifying your triggers, finding effective stress management techniques, building resilience, and incorporating relaxation practices into your daily routine have equipped you to handle whatever comes your way.

As we reached the final chapters, you learned about maintaining your gains, preventing relapses, building a support network, and planning for the future. You discovered the importance of setting new goals, embracing your journey, and celebrating your progress.

Finding your passion and pursuing hobbies became a way to enrich your life and find joy. Sharing your story to help others raises awareness and reduces the stigma surrounding OCD.

So, what's next? It's time to put all this knowledge into action. Continue to implement the strategies you've learned. Keep practicing mindfulness and ERP exercises. Set new goals and track your progress. Stay connected with your support network. Remember, this journey is ongoing, and every step you take brings you closer to a life where OCD doesn't hold you back.

You have the tools, the knowledge, and the strength to manage your OCD effectively. Celebrate your successes, no matter how small. Each victory is a testament to your resilience and determination. Keep moving forward, and don't be afraid to seek help when you need it.

If you're looking for more resources, I highly recommend exploring books like "When a Family Member Has OCD" and "Freeing Your Child from Obsessive-Compulsive Disorder." The International OCD Foundation (iocdf.org) is also a fantastic resource for information, support groups, and further reading.

I want to take a moment to thank everyone who contributed to this book and supported its creation. To the teens who shared their stories, your courage and honesty are truly inspiring. To the families, friends, and professionals who support those with OCD, your empathy and dedication make a world of difference. And to you, the reader, thank you for embarking on this journey with me. Your commitment to understanding and managing your OCD is commendable.

As a nurse and medical care clinician with a longstanding dedication to psychology and mental health, it's been an honor to share this knowledge with you. Remember, you are not alone. There is hope, there is help, and there is a path to peace and freedom from OCD. Keep moving forward, one step at a time, and never forget how strong and capable you are.

Dear Reader,

As I conclude "Break Free from Your OCD: A Teens Path to Peace and Freedom" I want to express my deepest gratitude for allowing me to be part of your journey. My hope is that the strategies and insights shared have provided you with valuable tools for personal growth and fulfillment.

In the spirit of community, I kindly ask for your support in one more way. If this book has resonated with you, please share your experience by leaving a review on the platform where you purchased it. Your honest review can guide others to find the support and strategies they need.

Writing a review is an act of kindness that can inspire others to take their first step toward healing. Your words can make a profound impact, helping to create a supportive community where people can learn, grow, and thrive together. Thank you for considering this request.

With heartfelt thanks,
Rick Bryant

ABOUT THE AUTHOR

Rick Bryant is an experienced Nurse and Medical Care Clinician with multiple decades of service and a longstanding dedication to psychology and mental health. Throughout his career, Rick has specialized in helping individuals develop and implement personalized care plans designed to enhance their mental, emotional, physical, and spiritual well-being. His work focuses on fostering self-esteem, promoting peace, and enhancing happiness in relationships and daily life.

In addition to his clinical practice, Rick is dedicated to extending his knowledge and insights to a broader audience. Through his writing and professional efforts, he aims to provide valuable resources and inspiration to those seeking guidance on their path to a more balanced and fulfilling life.

SUPPORT RESOURCES FOR OCD

Here is a list of U.S. national and international organizations that provide support for OCD, along with contact numbers where available:

U.S. NATIONAL SUPPORT FOR OCD:

1. International OCD Foundation (IOCDF)

- Phone: (617) 973-5801
- Website: iocdf.org

2. Anxiety and Depression Association of America (ADAA)

- Phone: (240) 485-1001
- Website: adaa.org

3. National Alliance on Mental Illness (NAMI)

- Helpline: 1-800-950-NAMI (6264)
- Website: nami.org

4. Beyond OCD

- Phone: (773) 661-9530
- Website: beyondocd.org

5. Peace of Mind Foundation

- Phone: (346) 701-8115
- Website: peaceofmind.com

∾

INTERNATIONAL SUPPORT FOR OCD:

1. OCD-UK (United Kingdom)

- Phone: 0333 212 7890
- Website: ocduk.org

2. OCD Action (United Kingdom)

- Phone: 0845 390 6232
- Website: ocdaction.org.uk

3. Anxiety Canada (Canada)

- Phone: 1-604-620-0744
- Website: anxietycanada.com

4. OCD Ireland

- Email: Use the website contact form for email communication.
- Website: ocdireland.org

5. ARFID and OCD Support (Australia)

- Phone: (07) 3254 1881 (Queensland)
- Website: arafmiqld.org

~

SUICIDE PREVENTION HELPLINES (GLOBAL):

1. U.S. National Suicide Prevention Lifeline

- Phone: 988 (U.S. only)
- Website: 988lifeline.org

2. Samaritans (UK and Ireland)

- Phone: 116 123 (UK and Ireland)
- Website: samaritans.org

3. Lifeline (Australia)

- Phone: 13 11 14 (Australia)
- Website: lifeline.org.au

4. Crisis Services Canada

- Phone: 1-833-456-4566
- Text: 45645 (Canada)
- Website: crisisservicescanada.ca

For a full list of global helplines, visit the **IASP Helplines Directory**: IASP Crisis Centres and Helplines.

These helplines offer immediate, confidential support for those in crisis.

REFERENCES

- *Obsessive-Compulsive Disorder In Children And Adolescents* https://www.aacap.org/AACAP/Families_and_Youth/Facts_for_Families/FFF-Guide/Obsessive-Compulsive-Disorder-In-Children-And-Adolescents-060.aspx
- *OCD vs. generalized anxiety disorder: Differences explained* https://www.medicalnewstoday.com/articles/ocd-vs-generalized-anxiety
- *I spent 20 years preparing for the coronavirus pandemic* https://www.bbc.com/news/stories-52564434
- *Cognitive Restructuring: Techniques and Examples* https://www.healthline.com/health/cognitive-restructuring
- *Externalizing OCD | Gatewell Therapy Center | Miami FL* https://gatewelltherapycenter.com/2018/09/10/externalizing-ocd/
- *Talking Back to OCD - ABCT* https://www.abct.org/books/talking-back-to-ocd/
- *Can Giving OCD a Name Help You Manage It?* https://www.treatmyocd.com/blog/can-giving-ocd-a-name-help-you-manage-it
- *An Action Plan for OCD* https://www.robertjamescoaching.com/an-action-plan-for-ocd/
- *Cognitive Behavioral Therapy for Obsessive–Compulsive ...* https://nyulangone.org/conditions/obsessive-compulsive-disorder-in-children/treatments/cognitive-behavioral-therapy-for-obsessive-compulsive-disorder-in-children
- *7 DBT Mindfulness Exercises to Help Control Your Emotions* https://mentalhealthcenterkids.com/blogs/articles/dbt-mindfulness-exercises
- *Acceptance and Commitment Therapy (ACT) for Teens* https://keyhealthcare.com/act-for-teens/
- *Managing OCD with the Triple A Response - NeuroLaunch* https://neurolaunch.com/triple-a-response-ocd/
- *Mindfulness and Cognitive Behavioral Therapy for OCD* https://iocdf.org/expert-opinions/mindfulness-and-cognitive-behavioral-therapy-for-ocd/
- *A Practical Guide to Meditation for OCD* https://www.verywellhealth.com/meditation-for-ocd-how-to-guide-5220556
- *Mindful Breathing | Practice | Greater Good in Action* https://ggia.berkeley.edu/practice/mindful_breathing

- *Mindfulness Exercises (for Teens) | Nemours KidsHealth* https://kidshealth.org/en/teens/mindful-exercises.html
- *Different CBT Strategies for Treating Obsessions in OCD* https://simplymentalhealth.ca/2024/04/20/different-cbt-strategies-for-treating-obsessions-in-ocd/
- *Cognitive behavioral therapy of obsessive-compulsive ...* https://www.ncbi.nlm.nih.gov/pmc/articles/PMC3181959/
- *Strides: Habit Tracker + Goals on the App Store - Apple* https://apps.apple.com/us/app/strides-habit-tracker-goals/id672401817
- *Why Celebrating Small Wins Matters - Harvard Summer School* https://summer.harvard.edu/blog/why-celebrating-small-wins-matters/
- *Study on the Interactive Factors between Physical Exercise ...* https://www.ncbi.nlm.nih.gov/pmc/articles/PMC8808202/
- *Effects of exercise on obsessive-compulsive disorder ...* https://pubmed.ncbi.nlm.nih.gov/36541901/
- *Nutritional psychiatry: Your brain on food* https://www.health.harvard.edu/blog/nutritional-psychiatry-your-brain-on-food-201511168626
- *Healthy Eating for Teens: What You Need to Know* https://www.healthline.com/nutrition/healthy-eating-for-teens
- *My OCD Story* https://www.mind.org.uk/information-support/your-stories/my-ocd-story/
- *DBT for OCD Relief: Proven Strategies for Lasting Change* https://counselingcentergroup.com/dbt-for-ocd/
- *Using Acceptance and commitment therapy (ACT)* https://www.youtube.com/watch?v=m-GDzh5GS40
- *Overcoming Obsessive-Compulsive Disorder (OCD) With ...* https://www.thrivehere.com/overcoming-obsessive-compulsive-disorder-ocd-with-exposure-and-response-prevention-erp-therapy
- *Families: "What Can I Do to Help?"* https://iocdf.org/expert-opinions/expert-opinion-families-what-you-can-do-to-help/
- *Managing OCD in Your Household* https://kids.iocdf.org/for-parents/managing-ocd-in-your-household/
- *How To Explain OCD To Someone Who Doesn't Have It - TX* https://dreamworkic.com/how-to-explain-ocd-to-someone-who-doesnt-have-it/
- *Everything You Need To Know About OCD in Kids and Teens* https://www.mcleanhospital.org/essential/ocd-kids-teens
- *Journaling for Mental Health* https://www.stanfordchildrens.org/en/topic/default?id=journaling-for-mental-health-1-4552
- *Mindfulness, PMR & Breathing Exercises for Anxiety Relief* https://www.

michiganmedicine.org/health-lab/3-easy-anxiety-relief-exercises-you-can-use-anywhere

- *OCD Thought Record* https://thinkcbt.com/images/Downloads/Thought_Records/OCD-THOUGHT-RECORD-THINK-CBT-V-09.07.18.pdf
- *13 Emotional Intelligence Activities, Exercises & PDFs* https://positivepsychology.com/emotional-intelligence-exercises/
- *Common OCD Triggers and How to Cope with Them* https://www.healthline.com/health/ocd/ocd-triggers
- *Stress Management and Teens* https://www.aacap.org/AACAP/Families_and_Youth/Facts_for_Families/FFF-Guide/Helping-Teenagers-With-Stress-066.aspx
- *Building Resilience in Teens: A Therapeutic Approach* https://serenitywellnessandcounseling.com/building-resilience-in-teens-a-therapeutic-approach/
- *Self-Help Strategies for Living With OCD* https://www.verywellmind.com/ocd-self-help-2510625
- *Clinical Practice Guidelines for the Management of ...* https://www.ncbi.nlm.nih.gov/pmc/articles/PMC6345139/
- *Relapse Prevention in the Treatment of OCD* https://iocdf.org/expert-opinions/expert-opinion-relapse-prevention/
- *Guide to Starting a Support Group* https://iocdf.org/ocd-finding-help/supportgroups/how-to-start-a-support-group/
- *13 SMART Goals Examples for Overcoming Your OCD* https://successindepth.com/smart-goals-for-ocd/

.

Milton Keynes UK
Ingram Content Group UK Ltd.
UKHW031323271124
451618UK00008B/307